2nd Edition

100
THINGS TO DO IN
ALBUQUERQUE
BEFORE YOU
DIE

D0711058

Deer dancer at Indian Pueblo Cultural Center

100

THINGS TO DO IN
ALBUQUERQUE
BEFORE YOU
DIE

2nd Edition

ASHLEY M. BIGGERS

REEDY PRESS

Library of Congress Control Number: 2018936115

ISBN: 9781681061436

Design by Jill Halpin

Printed in the United States of America
18 19 20 21 22   5 4 3 2 1

Please note that websites, phone numbers, addresses, and company names are subject to change or cancellation. We did our best to relay the most accurate information available, but due to circumstances beyond our control, please do not hold us liable for misinformation. When exploring new destinations, please do your homework before you go.

DEDICATION

To my mom, Kelley McCausland, who taught me that, in my
hometown, there's always something new to discover.

CONTENTS

Music and Entertainment

• •

Sports and Recreation

• •

Culture and History

• •

Shopping and Fashion

• •

• •

PREFACE

I'm one of the rare Albuquerqueans who was born, raised, and lives in my hometown. I love that the Duke City—whether through the film industry, Sandia National Laboratories, Kirtland Air Force Base, University of New Mexico, or myriad other reasons—beckons people from across the United States and the world. In some cases, these transplants explore more of the city than locals. I've met many Albuquerqueans who comment that there's nothing to do here. I, for one, never have enough time for all the places I want to go and events I want to attend.

When I began writing *100 Things to Do in Albuquerque Before You Die*, I wanted to capture all the enthralling aspects of the city I love, from the obvious picks to the offbeat ones. Yes, you'll find the Sandia Peak Tramway, Old Town, and the Isotopes in this guide, but I hope you'll also discover the unexpected, quirky, and cultural places and happenings that make the Duke City such a dynamic place.

This list isn't meant to be rankings from first to worst. Instead, it's meant to be a collection of 100 things that will give you insight into Albuquerque—and inspire you to keep exploring. Beyond the full list, you'll also find seasonal itineraries and ones for several interest areas, including locavores, families, and outdoor enthusiasts. Because Albuquerque sits in the heart of New Mexico, I've also included a few road trips that will take you beyond the city limits to explore this matchless region.

If there are Albuquerque musts I haven't mentioned here, let me know on Facebook at facebook.com/100ThingsABQ. I want to hear from you!

I hope your adventures are *all* good! Bueno, bye.

—Ashley M. Biggers

Bizcochitos

FOOD AND DRINK

CHOW DOWN
ON A GREEN-CHILE CHEESEBURGER
AT HOLY COW

Barbecue is to Texas as green-chile cheeseburgers are to New Mexico. This down-home classic is synonymous with the state. Every local has his or her favorite burger joint, and there are many competition-worthy plates. Each September there's a burger battle royale at the New Mexico State Fair, and New Mexico Department of Tourism even created a Green-Chile Cheeseburger Trail, so those hankering for gooey chile and cheese can get their burger fixes in every corner of the Land of Enchantment. Holy Cow Burgers serves Albuquerque's best gourmet version in a laid-back ambiance. The burger starts with a toasted bun made locally, then it's piled high with a thick patty of New Mexico–grown beef grilled to juicy perfection, roasted green chile, cheddar cheese, and all the fixings. Add the pecan wood–smoked bacon for a tough-to-beat dish. Add hand-cut fries on the side (just like mom makes) and a chocolate shake for the full mouthwatering meal. For vegetarians, the eatery also serves a tasty No Cow Burger, with a roasted eggplant and chickpea patty topped with miso aioli. It has the texture and flavor so many veggie patties lack. Add on cheese and green chile and the No Cow Burger becomes a dish even meat eaters will crave.

700 Central Ave. S.E., (505) 242-2991, holyburgernm.com

Neighborhood: EDo
*Kid Friendly

DRIZZLE HONEY
ON A SOPAIPILLA AT CASA DE BENAVIDEZ

Honey dripping down your fingers and arms is a sure sign you're enjoying Casa de Benavidez's sopaipillas—puffs of dough fried to crispy perfection that double as the state's unofficial dessert by concluding meals at New Mexican restaurants. Paul and Rita Benavidez founded this North Valley eatery more than fifty years ago. The restaurant grew from a takeout business to a full-fledged restaurant that eventually overtook the family's rambling adobe home—thanks in no small part to their spectacular sopaipillas and specialty sopaipilla burger. The restaurant, which offers serene patio dining beneath cottonwood trees during the summer, also serves savory versions stuffed with fajita meat, *carne adovada*, beef, beans, or *chicharrónes* (fried pork rinds). Still, the classic sopaipilla slathered in honey can't be beat.

8032 Fourth St. N.W., (505) 898-3311, casadebenavidez.com

Neighborhood: North Valley
*Kid Friendly

TIP
Although it's not officially on the morning menu, ask your server for a stuffed sopaipilla. The breakfast version is filled with scrambled eggs, hash browns, and cheese and topped with red or green chile and more cheddar.

DINE
AT FRENCHISH

Jennifer James is in a class of her own as Albuquerque's top chef. For seven consecutive years (2010–2016), the James Beard Foundation named her a semifinalist for its Best Chef: Southwest award; no other Albuquerque chef has been so honored. The awards are considered the culinary equivalent of the Oscars, and she certainly serves star-worthy dishes. She's overseen a handful of Duke City restaurants and, to follow her passion for French cuisine, she opened Frenchish in 2017 with co-owner Nellie Bauer. James isn't classically trained, so the "ish" gives her an out to take creative liberties. The grand open kitchen running the restaurant's breadth lets diners see their modern dishes take shape. James follows seasonality, so the menu shifts but may include appetizers like fried brussels sprouts with beurre blanc sauce, beet tartar salad, or escargot prepared in puff pastry. Immaculate vegetarian dishes and refreshing spritzers (try the Nob Hill swizzle) are also featured on the menu. James pays homage to her locale with desserts like the chocolate burrito—ice cream wrapped in a crepe. Some dishes, like the pepper ice cream, might challenge taste buds. But trust her. You'll be glad you did.

3509 Central Ave. N.E., (505) 433-5911, frenchish.co

Neighborhood: Uptown

TIP

Although the fine-dining meals here are worth every penny, the restaurant also serves budget-friendly three-course dinners for $30 on Thursdays. Reservations are always suggested, but there are usually seats available on short notice at the chef's counter or dessert bar.

SIP A MARGARITA
FROM ZACATECAS

The margarita is the Southwest's signature cocktail—just as the mint julep is in the Southeast. Zacatecas Tacos + Tequila + Bourbon bar mixes the best 'rita. The house ZACArita is a perfect blend of sweet and sour. If you want a bit more sizzle, try the Chalchihuitl, which is mixed with poblano-infused tequila. The Ruby, with blood orange, is a personal favorite. And if the dozen or so menu options don't appeal to you, you can build your own by choosing your favorite tequila and liqueur, or sample a tequila flight. If you need something to wash down your cocktail, this joint also has tasty tacos. James Beard Award–winning chef Mark Kiffin was inspired to open the casual restaurant after tasting Mexican street tacos. With New Mexico native Rodney Estrada as executive chef, they create upscale takes on the humble taco. Tacos aren't just for Tuesday anymore, and Zacatecas serves enough versions for every day of the week.

3423 Central Ave. N.E., (505) 255-8226, zacatecastacos.com

Neighborhood: Nob Hill

TEAR OFF A PIECE
OF A FRONTIER SWEET ROLL

Frontier Restaurant has been an Albuquerque institution since it opened in 1971. The budget-friendly eatery serves ample plates to hungry college students from the University of New Mexico, which is just across Central Avenue. But postgraduate diners eat here too, and locals have voted it the best place for late-night eats and cheap eats in alt-weekly reader polls. The barn-like restaurant is open from 5 a.m. to 1 a.m., seven days a week, which means you can order signature dishes such as green-chile stew, homemade flour tortillas, and *carne adovada* nearly any time of day. The menu's apex, however, is the sweet roll, which was featured on the Travel Channel's *Man v. Food*. The pastry's cinnamon folds are coated with sugar and drenched with butter, making them as crave-worthy as anything you'll ever eat. So grab a table near a portrait of John Wayne (the owners have an affinity for portraits of the Duke) and pull off an edge of the roll's spiral. They're also available at the four Golden Pride restaurants, which owners Larry and Dorothy Rainosek also operate.

2400 Central Ave. S.E., (505) 266-0550, frontierrestaurant.com

Neighborhood: University
*Kid Friendly

BREAKFAST
AT BARELAS COFFEE HOUSE

Rachael Ray dined at this eatery for her Food Network show *$40 a Day*, giving a nod to the restaurant's affordable menu. However, you're more likely to find neighborhood residents dining here than celebrity chefs. Brothers James and Michael Gonzales opened the eatery in 1978, and their sister Benita Villaneuva joined them quickly thereafter. Their family has lived in the Barelas neighborhood, one of the city's oldest, for four generations, and the restaurant is a testament to the family's longtime connections there. At Barelas Coffee House, servers know the names of every *vecino* (neighbor) and regular who enters the casual diner's doors. Movers and shakers meet here for out-of-the-office dealmaking. Local publications' readers' polls regularly acknowledge the cuisine here as city favorites, including huevos rancheros deliciously smothered in chile and authentic dishes such as menudo (a traditional soup made with beef tripe).

1502 Fourth St. S.W., (505) 843-7577, facebook.com/Barelas-Coffee-House-159362317607088

Neighborhood: Barelas
*Kid Friendly

PICK BERRIES
AT HEIDI'S RASPBERRY FARM

Heidi's raspberry jam—or, even better, raspberry red-chile jam—is a staple in Albuquerqueans' pantries. Founder Heidi Eleftheriou planted her first raspberry bushes in Corrales in 2000. With the plants overflowing, she began selling berries and jam at her flower stand at the Corrales Growers Market. The business blossomed and now operates out of a three-thousand-square-foot warehouse space in Albuquerque's Brewery District to meet the multistate demand. In season, fresh berries are widely available at local farmers markets. However, there's little better than tasting the tart, luscious fruit straight from the hedges. After a brief hiatus, Eleftheriou welcomed visitors back to the Corrales farm in 2017 to pick their own raspberries and now blackberries.

600 Andrews Ln., Corrales, (505) 898-1784, heidisraspberryfarm.com

Neighborhood: Corrales
*Kid Friendly

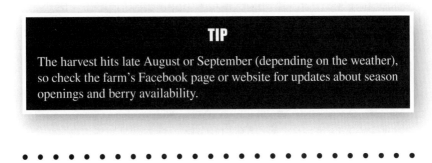

TIP
The harvest hits late August or September (depending on the weather), so check the farm's Facebook page or website for updates about season openings and berry availability.

DINE
AT PUEBLO HARVEST CAFE

Ensconced in the Indian Pueblo Cultural Center, this noteworthy restaurant is off the radar even of many locals. It should top lists, not fall off them. Chef Brent Moore is helping new Native American cuisine gain a popular foothold by incorporating traditional Pueblo flavors into contemporary cooking. Brunch brings pancakes made with blue corn and piñon, two significant Pueblo cooking ingredients. The whipped cream for the pumpkin sage french toast is kissed with sumac—an ingredient that can be foraged from the New Mexico high desert. Dinner leans traditional with wild fish and game–based dishes. Standouts include bison Poyha (a traditional Native American meatloaf) accompanied by blue-corn dumplings and fruit compote. Hazruquive stew simmers local white hominy and roasted yellow corn. For dessert, don't miss the pre-contact pumpkin pudding with agave-roasted pumpkin, candied pistachios, and ginger glass—a molecular gastronomical presentation of the root. With its ever-expanding Resilience Garden—a plot using traditional Pueblo farming methods—growing across the parking lot, Pueblo Harvest Cafe is increasingly becoming a farm-to-table restaurant.

2401 Twelfth St. N.W., (505) 724-3510, puebloharvestcafe.com

Neighborhood: North Valley
*Kid Friendly

TIP

The restaurant hosts live music every weekend year-round, with pizza fresh from the *horno* (a traditional oven). During summer, the Party on the Patio is one of the top happy hours in town.

SIP BUBBLY
FROM GRUET

Although wine is now produced in all fifty states, few can claim this accolade: New Mexico is the oldest wine-producing region in the country—yes, even before California. Franciscan monks planted the first grapevines here in 1629, near Socorro, just south of Albuquerque. European mission grapes are still grown in the state today, though most Duke City–area vintners stick to varietals more pleasing to the contemporary palate. Founded in 1984 by Gilbert Gruet and now overseen by his children, Laurent and Nathalie Gruet (head winemaker and company president, respectively), Gruet Winery is one of the state's marquee vintners. It's earned numerous awards; in 2011, *Wine Spectator* named the Gruet NV Blanc de Noirs a top 100 wine in the world—a particular coup since the sparkling wine costs less than $20. Although Gruet is internationally known for its *méthode champenoise* sparkling wines, it also produces still wines, including the noteworthy rosé created in partnership with Tamaya Vineyard. Owned by Santa Ana Pueblo, Tamaya Vineyard is one of the only Native American–owned commercial vineyards in the country and is the only one grown from scratch by a tribe.

Tasting Room: 8400 Pan American Freeway N.E.
(505) 821-0055, gruetwinery.com

Neighborhood: Northeast Heights

NIBBLE A BIZCOCHITO
AT GOLDEN CROWN PANADERIA

New Mexico's official state cookie, the bizcochito, is an anise-flavored, cinnamon-sugar number traditionally served at Christmas. Golden Crown Panaderia makes some 2,500 dozen each holiday season, but the Old Town neighborhood bakery makes them by hand year-round. Pratt Morales opened the bakery in 1972; today, he runs it with his son, Chris, who grew up baking alongside his father. When you walk into the adobe building bedecked with murals of hollyhocks, a server will hand you a crumbly bizcochito to eat while you're sifting through the array of treats on the menu. For a gluten-free option, choose the blue-corn version. Golden Crown also serves sweet and savory empanadas, spicy chile bread, and made-to-order pizzas.

1103 Mountain Rd. N.W., (505) 243-2424, goldencrown.biz

Neighborhood: Old Town
*Kid Friendly

TOAST THE CITY
FROM LEVEL 5

Hotel Chaco, Albuquerque's newest luxury hotel and the first newly built hotel near Old Town in decades, has quickly become a go-to spot for its rooftop restaurant and lounge. Hotel designers drew inspiration from the great houses now protected as Chaco Culture National Historical Park for the building's atmosphere and finishes. Gilbert Aragon, executive chef at Hotel Albuquerque at Old Town (Hotel Chaco's neighbor), and Mark Miller, of the iconic Coyote Cafe in Santa Fe, also found inspiration in indigenous culture for Level 5's changing menu. Previous menu standouts include cured venison with herb salad, wild blueberries, piñon, and juniper mustard; and three sisters vegetables (corn, beans, and squash—a significant combination among New Mexico's tribes and pueblos) with mint and pomegranate. Beverages also hint at the hotel's prevailing inspiration—take the Rio Chaco, which draws its name from the arroyo that once sustained Chaco Canyon. From the swanky hotel's fifth-story roost, diners can take in panoramic views of the Sandia Mountains, Old Town, and downtown. During October's Albuquerque International Balloon Fiesta, it's also a prime balloon-viewing perch.

2000 Bellamah Ave. N.W., (505) 318-3998, hotelchaco.com

Neighborhood: Sawmill District

OTHER ROOFTOP BARS OF NOTE

Apothecary Lounge (at Hotel Parq Central)
This top-floor bar serves panoramic views
of the Sandia Mountains and downtown
alongside Prohibition-era cocktails.
806 Central Ave. S.E., (505) 242-0040, hotelparqcentral.com

Ibiza (at Hotel Andaluz)
This second-story bar offers secluded tables
and lounge-worthy couches with views of
downtown and the Sandia Mountains.
125 Second St. N.W., (505) 242-9090, hotelandaluz.com

Seasons Rotisserie & Grill
This Old Town cantina serves killer cocktails
and live music.
2031 Mountain Rd. N.W., (505) 766-5100, seasonsabq.com

BITE
INTO BUFFETT'S CANDIES

Albuquerqueans go nuts—pardon the pun—for the piñon candies at Buffett's. George Buffett started the candy company in 1956 and the family still operates the business today. Bedecked with a candy-cane sculpture, the red-and-white building has become a city landmark, beckoning sweet-toothed locals for nut confections made with the small, buttery piñons native to New Mexico (including toffee, rolls, pralines, and brittles).

7001 Lomas Blvd. N.E., (505) 265-7731, buffettscandies.com

Neighborhood: Uptown
*Kid Friendly

TAKE FIELD-TO-FORK
TO THE NEXT LEVEL AT FARM & TABLE

When residential development threatened to overtake North Valley farm fields, Cheri Montoya's father, David, snapped up the fertile land. When Montoya, who already ran a shop in an adobe on-site, decided to become a serial entrepreneur, she launched Farm & Table to preserve the Rio Grande valley's agricultural heritage. Diners sitting inside the intimate restaurant or on its patio (the place to be on summer nights) can see the twelve acres of fields where much of their dinner is grown. When ingredients can't come from the resident farm, Sol Harvest, Montoya and executive chef Carrie Eagle work with a slew of local farmers and purveyors. In season, upward of eighty percent of the menu's ingredients are grown locally. The New American dishes let ingredients shine. Although menus shift with the seasons, previous editions have highlighted pan-seared rainbow trout with greens and poblano crema, and winter squash ravioli with mushroom and piñon. Don't miss the restaurant's eclectic global wine list.

8917 Fourth St. N.W., (505) 503-7124, farmandtablenm.com

Neighborhood: North Valley
*Kid Friendly

TIP
Farm & Table is set in a quaint adobe with limited seating. Be sure to make a reservation, particularly on weekend evenings and special occasions. Check the restaurant's calendar for wine dinners, yoga and meditation sessions, and its annual summer partnership with Tricklock Company—Theater on the Farm.

LIVE LIKE A LOCAVORE
AT CAMPO

Understanding Los Poblanos Historic Inn and Organic Farm's deep history enriches the dining experience at its newly expanded restaurant, Campo. Native Americans and Spanish and Mexican settlers long farmed the fertile fields along the Rio Grande now known as Los Poblanos. In the farm's modern history, Congressman Albert Simms and his wife, Ruth Hanna McCormick Simms, oversaw the land in the 1930s, launching Creamland Dairies (a staple on Albuquerqueans' grocery lists) and building a few of its architectural gems, including a cultural center designed by architectural icon John Gaw Meem. Today, Los Poblanos operates the cultural center, a fifty-room inn, a farm shop—which sells its eponymous line of lavender essential oil body products—and, of course, the restaurant. Housed in a renovated dairy barn and overlooking the lavender fields, Los Poblanos's restaurant sings with local, seasonal ingredients sourced from a dozen farms, including its own. James Beard Award–nominated chef Jonathan Perno crafts dishes that walk the line between rugged and refined. While menus follow the season, previous editions have included herb-stuffed chicken breast, potato gnocchi with squash and green chile, and mole amarillo with seasonal vegetables.

4803 Rio Grande Blvd. N.W., (505) 338-1615, lospoblanos.com

Neighborhood: Los Ranchos de Albuquerque

TIP

If your meal sparks star-chef aspirations, Los Poblanos offers one cooking class a month on topics such as bread making, cooking with honey, and desserts.

EXPLORE THE FRONTIER
OF BEER

New Mexico is the Frontier of Beer, at least according to the New Mexico Brewers Guild's apt tagline. While off the map of many beer connoisseurs (this is rapidly changing), the brewers here have had the freedom to experiment and push their flavors to new heights. This is particularly true in the Duke City, which has forty-four breweries or tap rooms in the area at the time of this writing. But it isn't just the quantity of breweries that makes this city a craft beer lover's paradise; it's the quality too. Several breweries, including Marble Brewery, La Cumbre Brewing, and Boxing Bear Brewing Co., have earned medals and top awards from the Great American Beer Festival and the World Beer Cup. Albuquerque is an IPA city—the working theory is locals' taste buds want flavors that stand up against our spicy New Mexican cuisine—so be sure to sample this variety in all its hoppy glory. However, the city follows all the top craft trends, so there are noteworthy taps for sours, Belgian-style ales, and many more to be found across town, including Tractor Brewing Co.

For more info: nmbeer.org

NOTABLE BREWERIES

Boxing Bear Brewing Co.

The Great American Beer Festival named this brewer Mid-Size Brewpub of the Year in 2016.

10200 Corrales Rd., (505) 897-2327, boxingbearbrewing.com

La Cumbre Brewing

The Elevated IPA is a crowd favorite and perennial award winner here.

3313 Girard Blvd. N.E., (505) 872-0225, lacumbrebrewing.com

Marble Brewery

Marble took home the coveted Small Brewing Company and Small Brewing Company Brewer of the Year award at the 2014 Great American Beer Festival, anointing it as one of the nation's best.

Downtown: 111 Marble Ave. N.W., (505) 243-2739

Westside: 5740 Night Whisper Rd. N.W., (505) 508-4368

Northeast Heights: 9904 Montgomery Blvd. N.E.
(505) 323-4030

marblebrewery.com

Tractor Brewing Co.

The craft creations here have knockout flavors, and the breweries are popular hangouts thanks to the hip vibes and packed community-event schedules.

Nob Hill: 118 Tulane Dr. S.E., (505) 443-5654

Wells Park: 1800 Fourth St. N.W., (505) 243-6752

Four Hills: 13170-C Central Ave. S.E., (505) 554-2462

getplowed.com

GRAB A TABLE
ON THE PATIO AT EL PINTO RESTAURANT

Burqueños can debate the best New Mexican food in town until, well, it's time for the next meal. El Pinto is usually in the running, but the restaurant's atmosphere helps it arrive at the front of the pack. It's quintessentially New Mexican with sprawling patios beneath hundred-year-old cottonwood trees, ristras hanging beneath portals, and the strains of mariachi music rising above the conversations shared over margaritas on the rocks. Members of the Thomas family have been serving their family recipes at El Pinto, or "the spot," since 1962, including most recently twin brothers Jim and John, who also began jarring the restaurant's signature salsa. The menu features a full—and tasty—complement of classic New Mexican dishes.

10500 Fourth St. N.W., (505) 898-1771, elpinto.com

Neighborhood: North Valley

TIP

On Sundays, the restaurant becomes a studio for YogaRitas. The margaritas flow before the class starts, which fosters a fun-loving atmosphere for the outdoor vinyasa session. Certified yoga instructor Sydney Fontaine Forestal—accompanied by her sidekick Tequila Barbie, a micro mini pig—leads the rollicking class.

CYCLE 'ROUND
TO BIKE-IN COFFEE

Albuquerque has a bevy of excellent coffee shops, but none offer the atmosphere of Bike-In Coffee, located at Old Town Farm. It welcomes visitors on Saturday and Sunday mornings to a food stand. There's just one catch: you have to arrive by pedal power. To preserve the farm's idyllic setting—and their relationship with neighbors—owners Lanny Tonning and Linda Thorne ask visitors to cycle to the farm. Founded in 1977, the farm's gardens have slowly been taking over horse corrals with rows of the three hundred varieties of produce they grow. After trucking seven hundred pounds of tomatoes to farmers markets for several years, they invited customers to come to them for produce and dishes prepared with their harvest. In spring 2018, Tonning and Thorne built a permanent structure to serve their clientele. Diners order at the counter as they did at the food truck that formerly housed the food operations, then pick a spot on the wraparound porch or in the garden to enjoy their meal. The hardest choice will be what to choose: savory mini-quiches, fruit pastries using the farm's raspberries or jujubes, or the crowd-pleasing "scookie"—a not-too-sweet, satisfying combination of a scone and a cookie. Food truck fans needn't worry; it will soon be transformed into an ice cream and *paleta* (popsicle) stand with farm-spun varieties like cucumber cooler, lavender plum, and carrot tangerine.

949 Montoya St. N.W., (505) 764-9116, oldtownfarm.com

Neighborhood: Old Town
*Kid Friendly

TIP

The farm sits at the nexus of the I-40 bike trail, the Paseo del Bosque Trail, Mountain Road (a bicycle boulevard where the speed limit for car traffic is eighteen miles per hour), and sleepy Montoya Street, providing a variety of routes to follow to the farm. Have a flat? Fix it at the on-site repair stand.

BRUNCH AT
THE GROVE CAFE & MARKET

This eatery is fresh—from the local, seasonal ingredients to the bright, light-filled setting. Jason and Lauren Greene have operated the bustling restaurant since 2006, serving salads, sandwiches, and breakfast items made from New Mexican produce, all-natural meats, and artisan breads and cheeses. For weekend brunch, it's prime mimosa-sipping territory. Don't miss the Grove pancakes—which are similar to French crepes topped with fresh fruit, crème fraiche, and local honey—and the pillowy English muffins. If you lean toward lunch, try the Farmers Salad with golden beets, Marcona almonds, and goat cheese or the Turkey Toastie sandwich with Havarti cheese pressed on whole wheat bread. Although most customers love the colorful macarons, for my money, the chocolate walnut cookie with sea salt is the best around.

600 Central Ave. S.E., (505) 248-9800, thegrovecafemarket.com

Neighborhood: EDo
*Kid Friendly

FUN FACT

Breaking Bad fans will remember this eatery as the setting where Walter White (Bryan Cranston) laced a packet of stevia with ricin poison to kill his former business partner, Lydia Rodarte-Quayle (Laura Fraser). The restaurant didn't actually stock the sugar substitute, but since it has received so many requests, you can now find packets at the coffee stand.

MELT FOR THE
CHOCOLATE CARTEL

In the hands of certified master chocolatier and chef Scott J. Van Rixel and brother Tim, chocolate becomes a fine art. Chocolate Cartel creations feature El Rey Venezuelan cacao, which makes up less than ten percent of the beans used worldwide, lending each truffle and bark an exclusive and refined flavor. Although Whole Foods and other major grocers stock Chocolate Cartel creations, visiting the company's Northeast Heights storefront is a trip to the mother ship. Rows of chocolate-covered almonds and toffee salt barks (its top seller) line the walls. Tiers of attractively decorated truffles are stacked in a glass case. Try the piquant smoked chile, filled with ganache seasoned with red chile, smoked salt, and vanilla, or the espresso, also filled with ganache, this one flavored with espresso from local roaster Moons Coffee & Tea. In recent years, the cartel has expanded its hold on Burqueños' taste buds with a line of gelatos, the most popular of which is the calorie-sin-worthy salted caramel.

315 Juan Tabo Blvd. N.E., Suite A, (505) 797-1193, chocolatecartel.com

Neighborhood: Northeast Heights
*Kid Friendly

PLACE YOUR ORDER
AT GREEN JEANS FARMERY

New Mexico's first shipping-container park has quickly become one of Albuquerque's favorite food spots. It's a next-level take on the food court with a trove of local restaurants operating out of the double-decker containers. Every member of your party can order something different here. Several places, like Rustic on the Green (home to great burgers), got their starts as food trucks but have found permanent homes here. Others, like Epiphany Espresso and Nitro Fog Creamery, which has the creamiest made-to-order nitrogen ice cream, popped up in this unique locale. Amore Neapolitan Pizzeria and Rockin' Taco (serving some of the best pies and street tacos in town, respectively) help complete the menu offerings. Santa Fe Brewing Co.—the state's original craft brewery—operates its only Albuquerque tap room here, and Broken Trail Spirits + Brew mixes tasty cocktails. Green Jeans is most popular in the summer thanks to its open-air approach, but there's indoor seating too, so don't cross this place off your list come winter.

3600 Cutler Ave. N.E., (505) 401-1000, greenjeansfarmery.com

Neighborhood: Midtown
*Kid Friendly

COME FULL CIRCLE
AT KARMA CAFE

This community-minded restaurant uses its revenue to provide meals for people who otherwise couldn't afford them. After observing a pay-as-you-feel restaurant model in Australia, Albuquerque native Wade McCullough turned his knowledge of the restaurant business into a food trailer, Food Karma, that still pops up at weekend growers markets. This stand allows customers to pay whatever they wish, or can afford, for staples like breakfast burritos. McCullough took the model to the brick-and-mortar Karma Cafe in November 2016. Although the café suggests a price for its breakfast and lunch dishes—try the veggie hash, biscuits and gravy, or curry—it still makes sure everyone has a nice meal using a voucher system. For those who rely on the boxed and canned fare of food banks, a fresh meal with the mostly local ingredients used at Karma Cafe is a rare treat.

1617 San Pedro Dr. N.E., (505) 312-8051, facebook.com/foodkarmaabq

Neighborhood: Northeast Heights
*Kid Friendly

JOIN
THE FOOD TRUCK CARAVAN

Albuquerque is firmly on the food truck bandwagon. These mobile eateries often turn up at local breweries, but to find a particular one, you'll need to check social media. You can also follow ABQ Food Trucks on Facebook for updates about the fleet. Here are a few top trucks: Street Food Institute doubles as a culinary training program for community-college students and budding entrepreneurs; it also serves gourmet tacos. Irrational Pie is a go-to for pizza. Kimo's Hawaiian BBQ serves dishes with island flair. My Sweet Basil and Good and Thorough Foods use seasonal, local ingredients for their homey fare.

facebook.com/abqfoodtrucks

Neighborhood: Citywide
*Kid Friendly

TIP
A changing lineup of food trucks gathers for lunchtime eats for Truckin' Tuesdays at Civic Plaza downtown and on Wednesdays in the parking lot of Talin Market in the International District. Both are prime spots to create your own buffet of food truck fare. Food trucks are also on hand for movie nights on Civic Plaza on summer Friday nights.

KiMo Theatre

MUSIC AND ENTERTAINMENT

GROOVE AT
¡GLOBALQUERQUE!

There are few festivals in the United States where world-music greats such as Calypso Rose and the Afro-Cuban All Stars play in the same time slot. (Calypso Rose is a prolific writer and songstress, most popularly of calypso music. The Afro-Cuban All Stars recorded the legendary *Buena Vista Social Club* album and are noted for reviving classic Cuban *son* music.) These headliners may have hit the stage just one year at ¡Globalquerque!, but stars such as these are the norm, not the exception, at the two-day festival held each September since 2005. Since that year, ¡Globalquerque! has featured artists from seventy-five countries and across the United States, with ten bands performing each night on three stages. Most play cultural-roots music, often not in English, but that language barrier doesn't keep audiences from grooving at the National Hispanic Cultural Center, where the celebration is currently held. "World music is where the adventure is right now," says founder Tom Frouge. It's a major regional music fest that's not to be missed.

globalquerque.org

Neighborhood: Barelas

ATTEND AN EVENT
AT KIMO THEATRE

The KiMo Theatre is one of Albuquerque's most prominent architectural landmarks, but it's certainly no relic: the KiMo's schedule is teeming with events. Now listed on the National Register of Historic Places, the picture palace and vaudeville theater opened in 1927. Its architectural style, known as Pueblo Deco, fused Southwestern and Art Moderne influences, the latter of which was popular in the 1920s and 1930s. Upon its opening, Pablo Abeita, then governor of Isleta Pueblo, named the theater using a combination of two Tewa words interpreted as "king of its kind." The theater fell into disrepair in the 1960s, but the city of Albuquerque purchased and renovated the structure. Today, it screens films from the outdoorsy Reel Rock Film, hosts local TEDx talks, and presents folk music concerts beneath its proscenium arch. The building's distinctive design elements are as well known as what happens on stage: the mezzanine of the lobby features *The Seven Cities of Cibola*, a series of murals by painter Carl von Hassler depicting the mythical cities of gold whose legend initially drew conquistadors into the lands that became New Mexico.

421 Central Ave. N.W., (505) 768-3522, kimotickets.com

Neighborhood: Downtown
*Kid Friendly (depending on the presentation)

CELEBRATE
FIESTAS DE ALBUQUERQUE

Modern Albuquerque may not look it, but it's in the triple-centenarian club. Today's city was founded in 1706 and was named after the Spanish Duke of Alburquerque (thus inspiring the city's nickname). The Duke City celebrates its founding each April with—what else?—a party in Old Town, its original neighborhood where the first Spanish settlers constructed homes, businesses, and the parish church that still presides over the square's north side. The festivities celebrate each of the five phases of the town's history (Native American, Spanish, Mexican, territorial, and today) with the drumbeats of native dancers, a parade of the founding Spanish families, and the swirling skirts of Mexican folkloric dances. Join in activities such as piñata making or watch blacksmithing demonstrations representing the territorial era.

albuquerqueoldtown.com
cabq.gov/culturalservices/historic-old-town/fiestas-de-albuquerque

Neighborhood: Old Town
*Kid Friendly

DON'T MISS

Stop in San Felipe de Neri Church. When Albuquerque was founded in 1706, the first building erected was a church. Although not the original building, this house of worship has been in almost continuous use for more than three hundred years. The intimate Chapel of Our Lady of Guadalupe (404 San Felipe St. N.W. at Patio Escondido, chapelguada-lupe.com) is also worth visiting.

DISCOVER
WHAT THE CHATTER IS ABOUT

French composer Claude Debussy once remarked that "works of art make rules; rules do not make works of art." Chatter is the rule breaker—and maker—of Albuquerque classical music. Chatter presents Sunday concerts fifty weeks a year with iconic and contemporary classical works, as well as spoken-word poetry at Las Puertas, a warehouse space in one of the city's industrial neighborhoods. The stripped-down space, bedecked with a collection of stately doors, highlights musicianship. David Felberg and friend Eric Walters founded Chatter in 2002 to gain more conducting and composing experience. Chatter merged with the Church of Beethoven, which first made the Sunday concerts a city tradition, in 2010. Previous concerts have included works by Bach and Chopin, as well as compositions by modern unknowns that challenge even this sophisticated audience's ears. Arrive early to purchase a cappuccino, partake of the breakfast pastries Chatter volunteers prepare, or sign up for a chair massage performed during the program.

Performance Space: 1512 First St. N.W.
Tickets: chatterabq.org

Neighborhood: Wells Park

TIP

Each year Chatter also presents a handful of cabarets—chamber music performances in intimate settings with wine/beer and appetizers—and a couple of large-scale concerts at diverse locations, from the Albuquerque Rail Yards to the Albuquerque Museum.

GET SPICY
AT NATIONAL FIERY FOODS AND BARBECUE SHOW

Some like it hot. Burqueños like their chile scorching. Founded in 1988 by author and chile maven Dave DeWitt, the National Fiery Foods and Barbecue Show is the spiciest show of its kind in the world. During the three-day event in March, more than two hundred vendors sponsor booths, most offering tastes of food products. If you want to incite a bout between your taste buds and some of the hottest products on the market—and on the Scoville heat scale—this is your kind of event. The food show also grants Scovie Awards to the best-tasting seasonings, marinades, and condiments. Pick up a program so you can quickly navigate to award winners. The show also includes chef demonstrations from greats who can bring the heat.

fieryfoodsshow.com

Neighborhood: Northeast Heights

CELEBRATE PRIDE
OF PLACE AT SOMOS ABQ

Debuting in 2017, SOMOS ABQ celebrates the best of Albuquerque for one day. In its first year, the citywide festival took over an eight-block stretch of Central Avenue in the heart of downtown with a sprawling row of white tents sheltering local makers, food stands, and a local craft beer garden. Headlining music groups and acts from across the United States played a handful of stages, and artist installations—including one that resembled an urban park—sprung up from the asphalt-paved landscape. Doors to small businesses lining the route swung open. Tickets were purposefully affordable so community members of every stripe could attend. The team of organizers—five friends with an idea, plus fifty more who joined the committee—volunteered their time to showcase the city's tech, culture, food, nonprofits, and so much more. They have a multiyear plan to grow the event into a national draw.

somosabq.com

Neighborhood: Downtown
*Kid Friendly

FIND A SPOT
IN THE GRASS FOR ZOO MUSIC

Pack a picnic, grab the kids, and throw out a blanket on the lawn at the ABQ BioPark Zoo for the Zoo Music summer concert series. The likes of the Indigo Girls and Chris Isaak have played in the band shell, as have touring acts in pop-rock, Americana, folk, Latin, and jazz. Be sure to arrive early on most Fridays, when the concerts are held, to explore the sixty-four-acre zoo, where more than two hundred animals reside, including three different kinds of penguins in a new exhibit. Many of the animals are active at twilight; occasionally, you'll hear the lions singing backup with roars.

903 Tenth St. S.W., (505) 768-2000, cabq.gov

Neighborhood: South Valley
*Kid Friendly

SEE A PLAY
AT ALBUQUERQUE LITTLE THEATRE

The Albuquerque Little Theatre may be the oldest community theater group in the city, but its annual season of shows is fresh and lively. The season includes local productions of Broadway theatrical and musical hits, like *One Flew Over the Cuckoo's Nest* and *Grease*, and productions staged with families in mind, like *To Kill a Mockingbird*. Founded in 1930, the Albuquerque Little Theatre moved into its current home—designed by renowned architect John Gaw Meem and built by the Works Progress Administration—in 1936. The likes of Vivian Vance, who played Ethel Mertz on *I Love Lucy*; Don Knotts, of *The Andy Griffith Show* and *Three's Company*; and Bill Daily, of *I Dream of Jeannie*, have graced this historic stage.

224 San Pasquale Ave. S.W., (505) 242-4750, albuquerquelittletheatre.org

Neighborhood: Old Town
*Kid Friendly (depending on the show)

TIP
Albuquerque's theater scene is dynamic, particularly for a city of its size. To learn more about Albuquerque's more than forty theater companies and venues, visit abqtheatre.org.

GET YOUR KICKS
AT ROUTE 66 SUMMERFEST

There are a few happenings that bring Albuquerqueans out in force—and this block party is one. Central Avenue, aka old Route 66, closes to regular car traffic for this summer celebration. Nob Hill bustles with food vendors—including a Food Truck Rumble where the mobile eateries battle for bragging rights—crafts booths, beer and wine gardens, and three stages of live music. The event recalls Route 66's halcyon days with a classic car show and a Neon Cruise.

cabq.gov

Neighborhood: Nob Hill
*Kid Friendly

CATCH A PERFORMANCE
BY TRICKLOCK COMPANY

Albuquerque's resident theater company is also one of the city's best exports; it travels internationally to tour works it creates from scratch. The company's home is the Tricklock Performance Laboratory. That black-box space lives up to its name as the troupe develops and tests new plays in its Excavations series—staged readings of scripts that are then discussed among the audience members and the creators. This company is also the mastermind behind Revolutions International Theatre Festival, which brings global, cutting-edge theater to Albuquerque for three weeks each spring. Previous years of the festival have featured dance troupes from Armenia, a theatrical company from the United Kingdom, and an improv troupe from Austria.

110 Gold Ave. S.W., (505) 414-3738, tricklock.com

Neighborhood: Downtown

LISTEN TO JAZZ
AT OUTPOST PERFORMANCE SPACE

This no-frills concert venue is all about the music. Both a nonprofit organization and an intimate performance space, Outpost presents more than one hundred shows per year. National Endowment for the Arts Jazz Masters—winners of the most prestigious award conferred on such musicians—perform here frequently, including during the summer New Mexico Jazz Festival. Summer also brings an all-local jazz series featuring Dixie to bop. You'll hear other genres here too, including folk, blues, and experimental music. Depending on the concert, the space may be set up like a jazz lounge or a concert hall. Either way, the 160-seat house is an intimate venue where you can see musicians at their formidable bests. Outpost also hangs visual arts shows—usually to tie into performances—and hosts spoken-word poetry slams and amateur nights where locals can get their starts.

210 Yale Blvd. S.E., (505) 268-0044, outpostspace.org

Neighborhood: University

TIP

Paid parking is available alongside the building or across the street. Seating is first come, first served, so arrive early to find a good vantage point.

DRAW ANOTHER CARD
AT EMPIRE BOARD GAME LIBRARY

Take family game night to the next level at this Nob Hill shop, which stocks five hundred board and card games for guests to play. Opened in April 2015, this board game café has a family-friendly vibe in a neighborhood otherwise known for its shopping, dining, and nightlife. Longtime neighborhood resident Rory Veronda envisioned a place to gather sans alcohol. Instead, gamers gather around cups of locally roasted coffee and classic board games like Risk and Monopoly, as well as newcomers like Splendor.

3503 Central Ave. N.E., (505) 232-4263, empiregamelibrary.com

Neighborhood: Nob Hill
*Kid Friendly

SEE A SHOW
AT POPEJOY HALL

Broadway comes to New Mexico at Popejoy Hall, the biggest indoor performance hall in the state, and an elegant one too. This University of New Mexico concert venue hosts touring productions of *Wicked*, *The Book of Mormon*, and other hits. Speakers like David Sedaris and Ira Glass have graced the stage, as have Las Vegas headliner the Blue Man Group and New York export the Martha Graham Dance Company. Homegrown talent performs here too, including the New Mexico Philharmonic.

Redondo Dr. and Stanford Dr. (at the University of New Mexico Center for the Arts), (505) 277-9771, popejoypresents.com
Tickets: unmtickets.com, (505) 925-5858, (877) 664-8661

Neighborhood: University
*Kid Friendly (depending on the show)

Hiking in the foothills of
the Sandia Mountains

SPORTS AND RECREATION

THRU-BIKE OR HIKE
THE PASEO DEL BOSQUE TRAIL

The Paseo del Bosque Trail has earned a first-place finish in the hearts of Albuquerque's cyclists and runners as the city's premier multi-use path. The sixteen-mile trail runs between the city's north and south edges uninterrupted by car traffic and through the scenic Rio Grande bosque (forest). If you complete its entire length, you'll spot elephants, whose ABQ BioPark Zoo enclosure is visible from the path; public art at Tingley Beach; the Rio Grande Nature Center State Park; privately owned camels; and Canada geese at the Valle de Oro National Wildlife Refuge, the city's 430-acre urban bird sanctuary. There are access points (and often parking areas) at Alameda Boulevard, Paseo del Norte Boulevard, Montaño Road, Campbell Road, Central Avenue, Marquez Street, and Rio Bravo Boulevard.

(505) 452-5200
cabq.gov/parksandrecreation/open-space/lands/paseo-del-bosque-trail

Neighborhoods: South Valley to North Valley
*Kid Friendly

PADDLE
THE RIO GRANDE

Albuquerque and water sports go together like peanut butter and bananas—unexpected, perhaps, but delicious. The Rio Grande, the fourth-longest river in the United States, cuts a sinuous path through the city's heart—much to the delight of paddlesport enthusiasts. Kayaks and paddleboards, which sit high in the water, fare well in the sometimes shallow waters that flow through this stretch of river. Coasting along the placid waters, paddlers can see geese, coyotes, and beavers that come to float, drink, and dip in the Rio Grande.

Outfitters for Tours and Rentals in Albuquerque

New Mexico Kayak Instruction
(505) 217-2187, newmexicokayakinstruction.com

Southwest Wind Sports
(505) 350-7942, windsurfnm.com

Quiet Waters Paddling Adventures
(505) 771-1234, quietwaterspaddling.com

Neighborhood: Citywide
*Kid Friendly

HIDE BEHIND THE BLINDS
AT RIO GRANDE NATURE CENTER STATE PARK

Walking the riverside trails through the cottonwood forests at the Rio Grande Nature Center State Park, you can scarcely tell you're in the heart of a metropolitan area with more than a half million residents. One of New Mexico's thirty-four state parks, it preserves 270 acres of cottonwood stands, wetlands, and meadows along the Rio Grande flyway, making it a year-round destination for birders. More than 250 species have been sighted here, including sandhill cranes, bald eagles, and great blue herons, among others. Duck behind the blinds that border the Candelaria Wetlands and the Discovery Pond outside the visitor center to view the waterfowl discretely. Across a footbridge, three easy nature trails await: the Riverwalk Trail, a one-mile loop along the river; the Bosque Loop Trail, a 0.8-mile trail; and the Aldo Leopold Trail, which is dedicated to the grandfather of the conservation movement and leads to the Aldo Leopold Forest. In winter (when the cottonwood branches are bare), you might spot a porcupine slumbering in the trees. Throughout the year, you may also encounter beavers, cottontail rabbits, or coyotes.

2901 Candelaria N.W., (505) 344-7240, rgnc.org, nmparks.com

Neighborhood: North Valley
*Kid Friendly

TIP

The volunteer Friends of the Rio Grande Nature Center offer guided weekend bird walks, nature walks, and monthly twilight hikes. Check the schedule online to join.

WALK THE WIDE-OPEN SPACE

There isn't just wide-open space around Albuquerque, there's wide-open space within the city. In fact, Albuquerque has more parkland per capita than any other city in the United States (a total of more than 27,000 acres in twenty-seven city-owned tracts). The Open Space Visitor Center is a fitting jumping-off point for your explorations. The center has interpretive exhibits, an art gallery, and agricultural fields that draw an array of wildlife. (For the athletically inclined, there's also a weekend yoga class held at the center. Depending on the season, it may be held inside or out, but it's always offered with epic views of the Sandia Mountains or the gardens.) To get out on the trails, locals favor Elena Gallegos Picnic Area and Albert G. Simms Park in the foothills of the Sandia Mountains. A network of paths loops through the 640-acre park, wending through stands of piñon and juniper and unfolding into views of the Sandias (to the east), Mount Taylor (to the west), and the Jemez Mountains (to the north). From here, the trail network extends into Sandia Mountain Wilderness.

Visitor Center: 6500 Coors Blvd. N.W., (505) 897-8831, cabq.gov

Neighborhood: Citywide
*Kid Friendly

WING YOUR WAY
TO VALLE DE ORO NATIONAL WILDLIFE REFUGE

In 2013, Valle de Oro became the first urban wildlife refuge in the Southwest. Several years after official protection of the 570-acre plot in the South Valley, it still takes some imagination to visualize the land's transformation from its previous life as the Price Dairy Valle Gold Farms into the planned rolling topography, wetlands, salt grass meadows, and cottonwood stands. Already frequented by several hundred species of avian and mammalian wildlife, these features will further benefit and attract fauna to the oasis within the largely industrial and agricultural neighborhood. Visitors are welcome to wander the fields and walk along the sandy paths of the Rio Grande daily from 8 a.m. to 5 p.m. to observe the prairie dogs, hawks, and coyotes (among many other species) here. Guided tours are available by reservation, but another great way to visit is during the refuge's quarterly mini-festivals. Construction on the visitor center is slated to begin in 2018.

7851 Second St. S.W., (505) 248-6667, fws.gov/refuge/Valle_de_Oro

Neighborhood: South Valley
*Kid Friendly

COMPLETE
THE FIFTY-MILE ACTIVITY LOOP

Composed of a collection of multi-use paths, bike lanes, and bicycle boulevards—roads with bike lanes and eighteen-mile-per-hour speed limits—this loop circumscribes the city. The route officially starts downtown and travels through Old Town and the museum district before crossing the Rio Grande and trekking to the edge of Petroglyph National Monument. It then travels the Riverside Trail to the Paseo del Norte Trail, where it chugs to Balloon Fiesta Park. It keeps riders and runners puffing along as it climbs to the city's northern edge and traces the foothills of the Sandia Mountains via the Tramway Trail. It then circles back downtown. Along the way, it travels through many of the city's top neighborhoods, and there's ample opportunity for shopping, dining, and imbibing along the way. As of spring 2018, 47.2 of the 50 miles were complete with pathways and signs to guide the way.

cabq.gov/50-mile-activity-loop

Neighborhood: Citywide
*Kid Friendly

REJUVENATE
AT TAMAYA MIST SPA & SALON

File Tamaya under places that make you go, "Ooh." This resort, co-owned by Hyatt and the Pueblo of Santa Ana, nestles in the Rio Grande bosque. It offers plush accommodations, dining at the Corn Maiden restaurant, and golf at Twin Warriors. All are decadent, but none as much as the spa, where the surrounding land and Native traditions inspire its signature treatments. The Three Sisters Salt Scrub blends blue cornmeal, Anasazi beans, pumpkin seeds (all traditional Puebloan foods), and salts to exfoliate your skin. Combine that with the Prickly Pear Toning Treatment to moisturize, firm, and tone your whole body.

1300 Tuyuna Trail, (505) 867-1234, tamaya.hyatt.com

Neighborhood: Bernalillo

HIKE
LA LUZ TRAIL

Trekking La Luz Trail is a rite of passage for Albuquerqueans. The eight-mile trail (one way) climbs four thousand feet along its route from the foothills to the Sandia Mountains crest. Switchbacks will help you manage the steepness as the trail rises through piñon/juniper-dotted foothills to ponderosa forests. The views of the city and the Rio Grande valley below are worth the sweat. Once you've summited, you can descend the way you came or head over to the Sandia Peak Tramway departure area to glide back to the base (which, take note, will drop you off in a different parking lot than the one you started in). This is a strenuous trail that should only be attempted by those with the physical fitness to accomplish the hike. Visitors should take note that the trail's altitude ranges from seven thousand to more than ten thousand feet. Don't make the Albuquerque Mountain Rescue Council save the day because you've underestimated the trail's difficulty!

Cibola National Forest Sandia Ranger Station
(505) 281-3304, www.fs.usda.gov/cibola

Neighborhood: Northeast Heights

TIP
If you're a trail-running superstar, enter the lottery for a spot in the La Luz Trail Run. The Albuquerque Road Runners club sponsors this race each August. abqroadrunners.com

PACK
"THE PIT"

Albuquerque may be short on professional sports teams, but it's long on school pride for the University of New Mexico Lobos. Cherry-and-silver-clad basketball fans are particularly zealous when they fill every seat in the university's arena, nicknamed "the Pit" because its playing floor lies thirty-seven feet below street level. The Pit has a reputation of being one of the loudest venues in college basketball and a winning one—at least for the Lobos, who have won more than eighty percent of their games on their home court. The Pit has also hosted NCAA tournament games. It was renovated in 2010, and in 2017 it received a new formal name: Dreamstyle Arena. But to Burqueños, it will always be simply the Pit. Just remember: in this arena, everyone's a Lobo. Woof, woof, woof.

1111 University Blvd. S.E., golobos.com
Tickets: (877) 664-8661, unmtickets.com

Neighborhood: University
*Kid Friendly

GET KNOCKED OUT
WITH MIXED MARTIAL ARTS

Albuquerque has emerged as the clear winner in the cage match for the country's top mixed martial arts training destination. Coaches Greg Jackson and Mike Winkeljohn's training curriculum and eponymous Jackson Wink MMA Academy churn out UFC champions, including Albuquerque native Carlos Condit (who has held the title in the welterweight division), transplant Jon "Bones" Jones (the former light heavyweight champion), and Albuquerquean Holly Holm (the former women's bantamweight champion), to name three. More than sixty professional fighters train there, and the public can join submission fighting training classes too. If you want to watch rather than compete in the octagon, check out the schedule for Jackson's MMA series.

Train: 301 Dr. Martin Luther King Jr. Ave. N.E.
(505) 900-3947, jacksonwink.com

Neighborhood: Downtown

TRACE THE PAST
AT PETROGLYPH NATIONAL MONUMENT

Native Americans and Spanish settlers who have lived in the Rio Grande valley have left indelible cultural influences. They've left physical traces too—in the black volcanic rocks of Petroglyph National Monument, one of the largest such sites in North America. The monument, on the city's west mesa, protects more than seven thousand acres of land, which is dotted with these four-hundred- to seven-hundred-year-old markings. Boca Negra Canyon features three self-guided trails offering views of some two hundred markings of birds, snakes, spirals, geographic designs, and handprints. The more rugged 2.2-mile Rinconada Canyon Trail offers views of some four hundred petroglyphs, as well as the remnants of the volcanic eruption that created the landscape there.

Intersection of Western Trail and Unser Blvd. N.W.
(505) 899-0205 ext. 335, nps.gov/petr

Neighborhood: Westside
*Kid Friendly

SOAK
AT BETTY'S BATH AND DAY SPA

Betty's Bath and Day Spa is a wellness oasis within the urban landscape. The spa offers co-ed communal, women-only, and private soaking pools. Adobe walls and shade trees enclose the pools, giving them a faraway feel. Betty's prides itself on having the best massage therapists in town and lives up to its promise with deep-tissue, sports, pregnancy, Thai, and sinus-relief options. To maximize your experience, soak prior to a massage. Betty's signature spa treatment is the Dulce de Cuerpo, a full-body exfoliating treatment that begins with a soothing coconut-oil treatment, followed by hand and foot massages, then the namesake sugar scrub.

1835 Candelaria N.W., (505) 341-3456, bettysbath.com

Neighborhood: North Valley

SHRED
AT SANDIA PEAK SKI AREA

Sandia Peak Ski Area is the closest ski area to the city. Via the Sandia Peak Tramway, skiers can be on the slopes within fifteen minutes of the western base. Most, however, choose to drive to the Double Eagle Day Lodge, where a café, sports shop, and ski school await. The ski area receives an average of 125 inches of snow each year. Thirty runs are accessible via five lifts, with more than half of the terrain suiting intermediate skiers. Opening and closing dates depend on snowfall, but the season generally runs from late December through mid-March.

From Albuquerque, take I-40 east to Cedar Crest.
At Exit 175, head north on NM 14 to Sandia Crest Scenic Byway 536.
Follow the byway six miles to the ski area.
(505) 242-9052, sandiapeak.com

Neighborhood: East Mountains
*Kid Friendly

TIP

If snowshoeing and cross-country skiing are more your speed, you may do so along the Sandia Crest Trail. For sledding and tubing, opt for the Capulin Snow Play Area.

GLIDE ALONG
THE SANDIA PEAK TRAMWAY

If Albuquerque has an Empire State Building equivalent, this is it. The tram is easily the largest tourist attraction in the city and offers spectacular views of the Duke City and Rio Grande valley during the 2.7-mile ride from the foothills to the crest of the Sandia Mountains. At one point during the trip, the car hangs some one thousand feet above Big Canyon, at approximately the same height above the ground as the top of the Empire State Building. In 1966, the tram made its first voyage as a way to transport passengers quickly to the backside of the mountain, home to the Sandia Peak Ski Area. (The tram receives regular maintenance and safety testing, not to worry.) The cables for the tram pass through only two towers on the way to the top; the car dips and swings slightly after passing through each, usually eliciting a few gasps from passengers. The tram glides smoothly above granite rock faces, pinnacles, and spires, offering occasional views of black bears, mountain lions, and mule deer below. Astute observers may even spot the wreckage of TWA Flight 260, which crashed into the mountains on February 19, 1955. At the summit, first catch your breath: you're standing at 10,378 feet in elevation. Then, take in the eleven thousand square miles of views possible from this vantage point, including those of Mount Taylor, Cabezon, and the Jemez Mountains. Passengers may follow the Crest Trail through the ponderosa pine forests either north or south. For many hikers, the Kiwanis rock cabin, 1.5 miles out along the north Crest Trail, is both destination and turnaround point. A new restaurant is slated to open at Sandia Peak in May 2019, and pending Forest Service approval, a mountain coaster is planned for the backside of the mountain to give non-skiers the thrill of zipping down the mountain.

30 Tramway Rd. N.E., (505) 856-6419, sandiapeak.com

Neighborhood: Northeast Heights
*Kid Friendly

HIKE FOURTH OF JULY CANYON

This scenic canyon in the Manzano Mountains is the go-to for fall foliage that rivals the East Coast (albeit on a much smaller scale.) Picturesque year-round, the canyon's true fireworks—the fiery leaves of Bigtooth and Rocky Mountain maples—burst in late September to mid-October, when scarlet and gold envelop the trail. Fittingly, this route is quite popular during autumn; the remainder of the year, the trail is relatively untraveled. The full trail is a 6.1-mile out-and-back hike; however, leaf peepers can follow the trail for as long or short as they wish beneath the ruby canopy.

Cibola National Forest, Mountainair Ranger District
(505) 847-2990, fs.usda.gov/cibola

Neighborhood: Manzano
*Kid Friendly

SOAK IN JEMEZ SPRINGS

Getting to the village of Jemez Springs, sixty miles northwest of Albuquerque, is half the fun: you'll drive the Jemez Mountain Trail, a National Scenic Byway that traces the Jemez River past red rocks and sheer canyon cliffs into the Jemez Mountains. Once you've arrived in the hamlet, you can dip into healing mineral waters at the Jemez Springs Bath House or Giggling Springs. Giggling Springs' glistening turquoise pools on the river's edge blend the comfort of a resort and the experience of being in the open air. Outdoor adventurers crave the natural hot springs in the Jemez Mountains. There are two popular treks: From the Battleship Rock parking lot, a 3.5-mile hike (round-trip) leads to the McCauley Hot Springs, where warm waters will soothe any time of year. North of Jemez Springs, off NM 4, a short trail leads to the river and up to the smaller Spence Hot Springs, which keeps a constant temperature of ninety-five degrees.

Sixty miles north of Albuquerque, off NM 4, jemezsprings.org

Neighborhood: Jemez Springs

*Kid Friendly

Jemez Springs Bath House, 62 Jemez Springs Plaza
(575) 829-3303, jemezspringsbathhouse.com
Giggling Springs Hot Springs, 40 Abousleman Loop
(575) 829-9175, gigglingsprings.com

ROOT FOR THE
ALBUQUERQUE ISOTOPES

For professional sports in Albuquerque, head to Isotopes Park to watch the town's AAA baseball team, which has made its home in the city since 2003. Since 2014, the Isotopes have been a minor-league farm team for the Colorado Rockies. (The team was previously affiliated with other franchises.) An episode of *The Simpsons*, in which Homer protests the Springfield Isotopes' plans to move to Albuquerque by going on a hunger strike, inspired the team's name. The name fits, thanks to Albuquerque's connection to nuclear history. Orbit, the mascot, seems to have experienced some radiation; it's unclear if he's an alien, a dog, a bear, or all three. Regardless, he's quite friendly—and flexible. He joins Albuquerque yogis and yoginis each spring for a day of yoga at the park. During the season, there isn't a bad seat in the stadium. For cheap seats, opt for the lawn. Families with kids should head to the Fun Zone for rides and games. Check the schedule for games offering fireworks and giveaways. A note about the park dress code: Yes, Isotopes gear is in vogue, but so is Albuquerque Dukes gear. The Dukes were the city's team until 2000, and Burqueños still proudly wear the team's gear.

1601 Avenida Cesar Chavez S.E., (505) 222-4058, abqisotopes.com

Neighborhood: University
*Kid Friendly

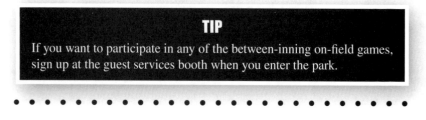

TIP
If you want to participate in any of the between-inning on-field games, sign up at the guest services booth when you enter the park.

HIKE KASHA-KATUWE
TENT ROCKS NATIONAL MONUMENT

The distinct volcanic formations here can be seen in only a handful of other places in the world, including Turkey, and they're in the Duke City's backyard. "Kasha-Katuwe" means "white cliffs" in the traditional Keresan language of nearby Cochiti Pueblo, but white is just one hue of the colorful cliffs and hoodoos at this national monument. The easy 1.2-mile Cave Loop Trail wanders among red-rock mesas; the 1.5-mile Canyon Trail treks up a narrow canyon to a mesa top offering views of the pumice and tuff pinnacles, some of which tower ninety feet, and the Sangre de Cristo, Jemez, and Sandia Mountains. In the arroyos, you may spot translucent obsidian (volcanic glass) orbs, another testament to the monument's geological past.

Fifty-five miles north of Albuquerque, off Indian Service Route 92
(505) 761-8700, blm.gov/visit/kktr

Neighborhood: Cochiti
*Kid Friendly

SETTLE INTO A LOW GEAR
FOR MOUNTAIN BIKING

New Mexico is fast becoming a top destination for fat-tire fanatics, but Albuquerqueans needn't go far to find some of the state's best trails. In the foothills, the Manzano/Four Hills, Elena Gallegos (especially along the 365 Trail), and Bear Canyon Open Spaces are all local favorites. All of the trails offer mostly dirt single track, with some sections of loose gravel and steep drops, and enough boulder sections to test your technical mettle. On the east side of the mountains, there are more grueling climbs— and rapid descents—on the steep Sandia Peak Ski Area trails, including King of the Mountain, the North and South Faulty Trails, and lower loops along trails such as Medio.

mtbproject.com

Neighborhoods: Northeast Heights and East Mountains
*Kid Friendly

WATCH THE SUNSET
AT VOLCANOES DAY USE AREA

When the sun sets over Albuquerque, it's difficult to decide where to look: to the multi-hued west, where the sun dips below the horizon, or to the east, to see the Sandia Mountains in alpenglow. Light glinting off the potassium feldspar in the granite mountains give the hills their distinctive watermelon hue. (Sandia means "watermelon" in Spanish, though the mountains' name actually comes from the nearby Sandia Pueblo, not the fruit.) One of the best places to watch the sunset is from the Volcanoes Day Use Area, part of Petroglyph National Monument. There you can hike loop trails up the three sister volcanoes that dot the western mesa (JA, Black, and Vulcan), each offering spectacular city and mountain views.

Off Atrisco Vista Blvd., (505) 899-0205, nps.gov/petr

Neighborhood: Westside
*Kid Friendly

TIP
If you plan to watch the sunset from the Volcanoes Day Use Area, be sure to leave your car outside the park gates. The parking lot is closed—and the gate locked—promptly at 5 p.m.

TAKE AN
OTHERWORLDLY WALK
AT OJITO WILDERNESS AREA

One of the two wilderness areas in Albuquerque's immediate orbit, Ojito is the harder to love. Badlands, steep mesas, and box canyons make up the landscape here—quite austere compared to the forested surroundings at Sandia. However, the bands of rust, ochre, and alabaster shale make this eleven-thousand-acre landscape imminently tantalizing. Follow two trails for your explorations: the Seismosaurus Trail through arroyos and across mesa tops for views, and the Hoodoo Trail, which wends among marbled pinnacles.

Sixty miles northwest of Albuquerque, off US 550
505-761-8700, blm.gov

Neighborhood: Outside of Bernalillo
*Kid Friendly

TIP

Getting to the wilderness area trails requires travel down maintained dirt roads. Mechanized travel, including by bicycle, isn't permitted within the wilderness area.

Indian Pueblo Cultural Center

CULTURE AND HISTORY

CELEBRATE CULTURE
AT THE GATHERING OF NATIONS
POWWOW

During the grand entry to this competition powwow each April, a drumbeat announces the presence of three thousand Native people streaming into Tingley Coliseum at Expo New Mexico. The singers' voices rise above even the jingling, pounding footsteps of the dancers who swirl in colorful regalia. Participants, who hail from some five hundred tribes in the United States, Canada, and Mexico, preserve their traditional cultures and share them with fifteen thousand attendees through dances like jingle, fancy, grass, and eagle. The powwow also includes the Miss Indian World pageant, a horse-and-rider regalia parade, and an Indian Traders Market, where you'll find everything from cone jingles for fancy-dance dresses to Navajo jewelry. Traditional and contemporary Native musicians play at Stage 49, with groups ranging from rock to hip-hop.

(505) 836-2810, gatheringofnations.com

Neighborhood: Midtown
*Kid Friendly

SHOUT ¡OLÉ!
AT TABLAO FLAMENCO ALBUQUERQUE

Albuquerque's distinctive flamenco scene is an inheritance of its Spanish culture. The National Institute of Flamenco has preserved the dance and music's artistry for decades with classes, performances, and festivals. The art now has a permanent venue with Tablao Flamenco, a dedicated space within Hotel Albuquerque. The intimate space presents nearly nightly performances as flamenco was meant to be seen—with guests gathered around tables sipping sangria, munching on tapas, and enjoying performances just steps away. The cante flamenco (song) and toque (playing of the guitar) reverberate around a couple dozen tables as the dancers articulate every emotional nuance of the passionate art with twirls of their hands, swishes of fringed skirts, and stomps of their feet.

Hotel Albuquerque
800 Rio Grande Blvd. N.W., (505) 222-8797, tablaoflamenco.org

Neighborhood: Old Town

TIP
The National Institute of Flamenco hosts the Festival Flamenco Internacional de Alburquerque each June. Regarded as the longest-standing flamenco event outside of Spain, the weeklong event draws talents from around the globe for public performances and master classes. nationalinstituteofflamenco.org

WATCH A MATACHINES DANCE
AT JEMEZ PUEBLO

Watching a Matachines dance is an only in New Mexico experience. (Although the dance is performed other places, the state's villages and tribes have given it their own unique twists.) The masked dance tells the story of conquest. The characters include a monarch, masked captains, La Malinche (an Indian woman who had a relationship with Hernán Cortés), El Toro (the bull, who may also symbolize the Devil, depending on the interpretation), and the Abuelo (grandfather) and Abuela (grandmother). Around Albuquerque, you can see the traditional dance performed each August as part of the festivities at Las Fiestas de San Lorenzo in Bernalillo and each January 1 at Jemez Pueblo, both north of Albuquerque. Jemez Pueblo performs both the Hispanic and Native American versions of the dance, for which participants wear different regalia and tell slightly different versions of the story.

townofbernalillo.org, jemezpueblo.org

Neighborhoods: Bernalillo and Jemez Pueblo

BROWSE THE NATIONAL
HISPANIC CULTURAL CENTER

This world-class center is one of a kind in the United States. It's the only center to celebrate Hispanic and all Latin American cultures under one umbrella. The sprawling campus includes a visual arts museum, several performance halls, an education building, and a genealogy center. The visual arts collection is a standout: The eleven-thousand-square-foot gallery space exhibits exciting contemporary and traditional works from renowned Latin American, Spanish, and Nuevo Mexicano artists, like Charles M. Carrillo and Luis Jimenez, as well as changing exhibits. It hosts some seven hundred events a year—from film screenings, to world-class music concerts, to art openings—so it's a rare night you'll find the center's calendar blank. No wonder it's become one of the top attended cultural institutions in the state.

1701 Fourth St. S.W., (505) 246-2261, nhccnm.org

Neighborhood: Barelas
*Kid Friendly (depending on the show)

TIP

Don't miss the Torreón (watchtower) at the entrance. Inside, *Mundos de Mestizaje* retells three thousand years of Hispanic history and has earned acclaim as the largest concave fresco in North America. The true fresco by Santa Fe artist Frederico Vigil took more than ten years to design and paint; Vigil used local models for his depictions of Toltecs, Mayans, medieval Spanish, and early Albuquerqueans, all of whom figure in the painting.

VIEW THE MURALS
AT CORONADO HISTORIC SITE

This monument is named for Francisco Vasquez de Coronado, whose entrada camped near Kuaua Pueblo (meaning "evergreen" in the Tiwa language) between 1540 and 1542 during its search for the fabled Seven Cities of Gold. When Museum of New Mexico archaeologists excavated the pueblo in the 1930s, they discovered a noteworthy kiva (ceremonial chamber). The ceremonial chamber is square (most are round). It also contained many layers of murals that are some of the finest examples of pre-Columbian art found in the United States; the murals were painted as frescoes in the fifteenth century. You can see fourteen sections of the original murals in the visitor center. With a guide or ranger escort, you can visit the square kiva where Ma Pe Wi, a Zia Pueblo artist, recreated the murals in 1938. They were restored in 2013. The frescoes depict soaring eagles and swallows, seeds, and life-giving raindrops.

485 Kuaua Rd., (505) 867-5351, nmhistoricsites.org/coronado

Neighborhood: Bernalillo
*Kid Friendly

SIT BACK
FOR FIRST FRIDAY FRACTALS

Your inner nerd can have a night out on the town at First Friday Fractals, a monthly show during which fractals swirl across the full dome of the planetarium at the New Mexico Museum of Natural History and Science. Fractals, both a natural and mathematical phenomenon, are repeating patterns that display at every scale, and these designs come to life in the domed presentation. The first show features original music and narration that describes the phenomenon. A second show, *Fractals Rock!*, plays at two later showings and offers a similar immersive journey with less explanation.

New Mexico Museum of Natural History and Science
1801 Mountain Rd. N.W., (505) 841-2800, nmnaturalhistory.org

Neighborhood: Old Town
*Kid Friendly

TIP
Buy your tickets in advance, as these shows typically sell out. Online ticket sales end at noon on the day of the show.

FLY HIGH
AT THE ALBUQUERQUE INTERNATIONAL BALLOON FIESTA

The Albuquerque International Balloon Fiesta is the city's largest sporting event and its most popular festival rolled into one. Balloon Fiesta, as it's known to locals, is also the largest hot-air balloon gathering in the world. In 2011, with 345 balloons taking flight, the fiesta set the record for the most balloons lifting off in an hour; usually, more than five hundred hot-air balloon teams attend the event overall. The nine-day fiesta, which is held annually the first week of October, features a variety of events throughout the week. The most popular are the morning mass ascensions, when attendees huddle in the dawn light—hot chocolate and breakfast burritos in hand—watching the balloons inflate and take off in waves from Balloon Fiesta Park. Balloons hover for a couple of hours, riding the drafts of the "Albuquerque box"—a weather phenomenon that keeps the balloonists aloft over the city for long flights and has helped establish the city's reputation as a flying destination. The Special Shapes Rodeos, with balloons in the forms of Yoda, Darth Vader, and others, are also favorites. During evening glows, balloons are tethered to the ground and fire their burners to light up the night sky.

5000 Balloon Fiesta Pkwy. N.E., (888) 422-7277
(505) 821-1000, balloonfiesta.com

Neighborhood: Northeast Heights
*Kid Friendly

TIPS

Although there's parking available at Balloon Fiesta Park, the best way to arrive is via the park-and-ride shuttle buses from satellite locations around the city. Or even better, come by bike; you can check your wheels at the bicycle valet.

Balloons Are Always in Burque: The Anderson-Abruzzo Albuquerque International Balloon Museum is open year-round and tells the history of the sport both around the globe and in town. Most enthralling are the original and replica versions of historic crafts, including the *Double Eagle II*, in which Albuquerque balloonists Maxie Anderson and Ben Abruzzo, along with Larry Newman, completed the first manned crossing of the Atlantic Ocean in 1978, and that of Troy Bradley (a local) and Leonid Tiukhtyaev, who set the world records for distance and flight duration in 2015. During the fiesta, you can enjoy breakfast or dinner at the museum and take in views from its balcony.

9201 Balloon Museum Dr. N.E., (505) 768-6020
balloonmuseum.com

GALLERY HOP
AT FIRST FRIDAY ARTSCRAWL

In 2015, ARTScrawls marked twenty-five years in Albuquerque. The citywide, self-guided gallery tour happens the first Friday of each month. On that day, participating galleries open new exhibitions and host artist receptions. Check the schedule online for details about specific shows. The galleries range from those presenting thought-provoking, contemporary creations, such as 516 ARTS, to those with more traditional fine art, such as Sumner & Dene.

artscrawlabq.org

Neighborhood: Citywide

SPEND AN EVENING
WITH THE BARD AT
SHAKESPEARE ON THE PLAZA

Grab a (free!) seat during the month-long run of Shakespeare on the Plaza, held on select dates in June and July. In 2014, the Vortex Theatre—one of the city's theatrical institutions—took its summer Shakespeare festival outside, staging everything from *The Comedy of Errors* to *A Midsummer Night's Dream* alfresco on Civic Plaza. In many ways, the move returned the plays to their roots, since during the English Renaissance they flourished at outdoor summer festivals. There's something magical about seeing Juliet pine over Romeo in the heart of the city against a skyscraper backdrop.

shakespeareontheplaza.org

Neighborhood: Downtown
*Kid Friendly (depending on the play)

TAKE A PUBLIC
ART WALK

Albuquerque boasts one of the oldest public art programs in the country. In 1978, voters passed the Art in Municipal Places Ordinance, which has erected some eight hundred works, including four hundred sculptures, murals, paintings, and mosaics in downtown alone. The Albuquerque Convention Center has a large collection of pieces within the building, and on the exterior students from the Mayor's Art Summer Institute at Harwood Art Center have created a mosaic over the course of more than a decade that tells the story of New Mexico's cultural history. Don't miss the following installations, which demonstrate the breadth of the collection: *Sidewalk Society*, by Glenna Goodacre, a collection of bronze statues at Third and Tijeras; *La Pared de Imágenes (The Wall of Images)*, by Byron Wickstrom, featuring forty-two individual metal sculptures, each with a distinct geometric form and patina; and *Auto Hawk*, by Christopher Fennell, a twenty-four-foot sculpture incorporating thirty car doors on Second Street. Find suggested tours and information about the individual works on the city of Albuquerque's website.

cabq.gov

Neighborhood: Citywide
*Kid Friendly

PHOTO OP

The "Chevy on a Stick" (created by Barbara Grygutis and officially known as *Cruising San Mateo I* before it earned its nickname in the early 1990s) is one of the city's most notable—and most controversial—public art pieces. The sculpture, in which a full-sized, tiled car sits atop an arch, has become a must-do photo op.

WATCH A DANCE
AT THE INDIAN PUEBLO
CULTURAL CENTER

In New Mexico, traditional Native American dances, which have deep cultural roots in each pueblo and tribe, are reflections of yesteryear and today. Usually, seeing such dances requires a road trip. It's well worth the drive, but in town you can head to the Indian Pueblo Cultural Center, where groups from different pueblos and tribes share this facet of their culture each weekend—and more often during peak times, such as during the Albuquerque International Balloon Fiesta. You may encounter the Olla Maidens from Zuni Pueblo, the Red Turtle Dancers from Pojoaque Pueblo, or buffalo dancers from Jemez Pueblo. The Indian Pueblo Cultural Center is unique in the world because it's collectively owned by the state's nineteen pueblos; the center is the preeminent place to learn about the pueblos' history, culture, and art. Beyond the dances, the museum presents a notable collection of Pueblo pottery, as well as baskets, weavings, paintings, murals, jewelry, and photographs. The permanent exhibit *We Are of This Place* tells the story of the Pueblo people from their perspective.

2401 Twelfth St. N.W., (505) 843-7270, indianpueblo.org

Neighborhood: North Valley
*Kid Friendly

SEE AN INDIE FLICK
AT THE GUILD CINEMA

The Guild is Albuquerque's independent film house. It screens all manner of low-budget and off-the-radar films, from classic cult hits to newly produced film festival darlings. Oscar-nominated shorts (animated, documentary, and live action) and full-length documentaries get their day on the big screen here during awards season. The Guild is also the home of the Sin Fronteras Film Festival, which is devoted to Latin American movies, and the New Mexico Italian Film Festival. The intimate house has only a few dozen seats, so arrive early to find one and get your popcorn. Don't miss the red chile powder topping.

3405 Central Ave. N.E., (505) 255-1848, guildcinema.com

Neighborhood: Nob Hill

PAINT YOUR FACE
FOR THE DÍA DE LOS MUERTOS Y MARIGOLD PARADE

Calaveras (representations of human skulls) come to life on the faces of the participants of the Día de Los Muertos y Marigold Parade. Held in honor of the Mexican holiday Día de Los Muertos, the procession through the South Valley features throngs of walkers and cars—from low riders to hearses—decked out in honor of the dead. Garlands of flowers, real and fabric, string across mock coffins and headstones, and puppeteers make eight-foot skeletons dance to the trumpets of mariachi music. The aroma of marigold flowers rises as parade participants sprinkle the golden petals as they walk. Everyone is welcome to participate (you must complete an application), or you can just watch. The parade funnels into a park where altars pay homage to friends and family members who have passed.

muertosymarigolds.org

Neighborhood: South Valley
*Kid Friendly

EARN A CERTIFICATE
OF BRAVERY AT THE AMERICAN INTERNATIONAL RATTLESNAKE MUSEUM

To earn your certificate of bravery here, you'll have to navigate an expansive collection of live rattlesnakes—a larger collection than even the likes of the National Zoo or the San Diego Zoo. Chihuahuan ridge-nose, canebrake, and tiger rattlesnakes are all on display in this conservation-minded center, as is snake memorabilia.

202 San Felipe St. N.W., (505) 242-6569, rattlesnakes.com

Neighborhood: Old Town
*Kid Friendly

TOUR *BREAKING BAD*
FILMING LOCATIONS

Breaking Bad, the TV drama that put Albuquerque on the pop-culture map, had locals asking if the show about a teacher turned meth cook made the city look badass—or just bad. Either way, the show, which was both filmed and set in the Duke City, continues to attract legions of fans on pilgrimages to visit the real-life locations that turned up on the AMC drama—even more than ten years after the show's finale. For a self-guided tour, see the following list of must-see filming locations. For a *Breaking Bad* experience through and through, hitch a ride on a Breaking Bad RV Tour. Actors and extras from the show lead the tours on one of the three 1986 Fleetwood Bounder RVs that appeared on the small screen. The ringing of Hector Salamanca's bell (a look-alike) marks the tour's departure to seventeen of the show's filming locations, including Tuco's office (on the second floor of real-life Java Joe's), Combo's corner (at Second Street and Hazeldine Avenue), the DEA offices (the agency's true-to-life whereabouts), and other must-see locations.

breakingbadrvtours.com

Neighborhood: Citywide

MUST-SEE FILMING LOCATIONS

Crossroads Motel
1001 Central Ave. N.E.

Dog House Drive-In
1216 Central Ave. N.W.

Jesse Pinkman's House*
Northeast corner of Los Alamos Ave.
and Sixteenth St. S.W.

John B. Robert Dam
On Juan Tabo Blvd. N.E.,
between Montgomery Blvd. and Spain Rd.

Mister Car Wash, aka A1A Car Wash
9516 Snow Heights Cir. N.E.

Walter White's House*
3828 Piermont Dr. N.E.
(Intersection of Piermont Dr. and Orlando Pl.)

Twisters, aka Los Pollos Hermanos
4257 Isleta Blvd. S.W.

*Please note: These are private residences. Stay on the sidewalk and be respectful of the owners' wishes and privacy. The owners of the real-life Walter White house even erected a fence around the property to keep fans at bay. Hey, you probably would too, after regularly having pizzas thrown on your roof.

FLY AWAY
TO THE SPACESHIP HOUSE

Okay, that's not the house's proper name. But that's what Burqueños call Bart Prince's residence and studio. Completed in 1984, this structure and its companion, also from the famed architect's portfolio, certainly look as though they flew right out of a sci-fi movie and into an Albuquerque residential neighborhood. Prince, who is known for pushing design boundaries, works in the cylindrical studio at the front of the property, just behind the earth berm. He designed the second (submarine-shaped) story to be heated via passive solar. The stone tower at the south end of the property was added in 1990 and serves as a library and storage area.

3501 and 3507 Monte Vista Blvd.

Neighborhood: Nob Hill

ALTERNATE BART PRINCE ARCHITECTURE SIGHTING

Bart Prince also designed the swirling spiral building, similar to that of a snail shell, at the entrance of Casas de Suenos (casasdesuenos.com), a bed-and-breakfast in Old Town.

EXPLORE
THE UNIVERSITY OF NEW MEXICO ART MUSEUM

Unless you're a university student, this museum may be off your radar. The two-story annex in the UNM Center for the Arts installs some of the best exhibitions in town. The museum has the 2,400-artwork Raymond Jonson collection, featuring pieces by Jonson, the founder of the Transcendental Painting Group, and many of his contemporaries, including Agnes Martin, Elaine DeKooning, Richard Diebenkorn, and Josef Albers. The museum also hangs a changing series of shows in photography, sculpture, painting, and even significant installations.

Redondo Dr. and Stanford Dr.
(at the University of New Mexico Center for the Arts)
(505) 277-4001, artmuseum.unm.edu

TIP

While you're on campus, check out the Maxwell Museum of Anthropology, where two permanent exhibits explore the ancient history of Southwestern peoples.

1 University Blvd. N.E., (505) 277-4405, unm.edu/~maxwell

VISIT THE PAST
AT ALBUQUERQUE MUSEUM

With the *Only in Albuquerque* history gallery, this gem is a repository of the city's past. The exhibit tells the story of the Rio Grande valley. The displays show Navajo and Pueblo blankets that double as historical artifacts and art, farm and ranch tools, and early European maps of New Spain. The museum's collection of helmets, swords, and colonial European armor is considered among the best in the United States. On Albuquerque's fertile creative grounds, history is woven with art. The creatives featured in the museum's permanent art exhibit, *Common Ground: Art in New Mexico*, reads like a who's who list of Southwestern art: it features the works of Ernest L. Blumenschein, Georgia O'Keeffe, and Fritz Scholder, to name a few.

2000 Mountain Rd. N.W., (505) 243-7255, albuquerquemuseum.org

Neighborhood: Old Town
*Kid Friendly

TIP

The museum offers free admission several times each month: every Sunday from 9 a.m. to 1 p.m.; the first Wednesday of the month from 9 a.m. to 5 p.m.; and the third Thursday of the month from 5 to 8 p.m. The third-Thursday events feature special programming (think Geeks Who Drink quizzes) and a light menu and cash bar at the museum café.

TUNE IN

The New Mexico Jazz Workshop teams with the museum each summer for Salsa and Jazz & Blues Under the Stars, with concerts (usually Friday and Saturday nights) in the outdoor amphitheater. nmjazz.org

FEEL THE GLOW
WITH LUMINARIAS IN OLD TOWN

Duke City denizens' favorite holiday tradition is seeing luminarias on Christmas Eve. These decorations may be modest (just paper bags weighted down with sand and a small candle lit inside), but the ethereal flickering of thousands makes the holiday merry and bright. The best neighborhoods to see them are Old Town and the Country Club, where businesses and residences line adobe walls and walkways with the lanterns. For the holiday, the city of Albuquerque turns its public buses into tour coaches to drive passengers through these renowned neighborhoods to see the lights while staying warm. Tickets for the tours sell out early—sometimes in one day. To ensure you get one, buy yours the day after Thanksgiving, when tickets go on sale. If you want to walk rather than ride, visit Old Town after 9 p.m. (my favorite time), when the crowds, cars, and buses have dissipated.

Luminaria Tour: cabq.gov

Neighborhoods: Old Town and Country Club
*Kid Friendly

DICTION DEBATE

Albuquerqueans refer to the bagged beauties as *luminarias*. However, in northern New Mexico, paper bags with a candle inside are called *farolitos* and small bonfires *luminarias*. Who's right? Whomever you're speaking to at the time.

GLOW UPSIZED

On Christmas Eve, a dozen pilots tether their hot-air balloons at Arroyo del Oso Golf Course, in the Northeast Heights, for a glow.

7001 Osuna Rd. N.E., (505) 884-7505, cabq.gov

SEE AN EXHIBITION
AT HARWOOD ART CENTER

As one of the most vibrant destinations in the city, there's always something happening at the Harwood. It's a lifelong-learning center and a wing of Escuela del Sol Montessori, which, along with the school and art spaces, covers a full city block downtown. The Harwood supports selected emerging artists through a professional development program and hosts a couple floors of art studios. Once a year, the artists open the doors to the public so they can enjoy works in progress. For the finished results, check out the Harwood's downstairs gallery space, which mounts a handful of curated shows each year. Bitten by the art bug? The Harwood hosts adult art workshops in everything from journaling to silversmithing.

1114 Seventh St. N.W., (505) 242-6367, harwoodartcenter.org

Neighborhood: Downtown

CRUISE
ROUTE 66

Follow the neon along eighteen miles of old Route 66 through Albuquerque. The historic Mother Road, now Central Avenue, bisects the city on its path from Chicago, Illinois, to Los Angeles, California. Along the way, you'll pass some of the city's most popular neighborhoods and attractions, including Nob Hill, a trendy shopping area; the University of New Mexico; downtown and Old Town; the ABQ BioPark Aquarium and Botanic Garden; and the volcanoes that hug the city's western edge. Take note of the intersection of Central and Fourth Street: Fourth Street was part of the original route (1926–1937) that ran north/south through Albuquerque along this existing road. In 1931, the route was realigned along an east/west trajectory. This is one of the few places that the two phases of the road intersect.

rt66nm.org

Neighborhood: Citywide
*Kid Friendly

TIP
For the full vintage vibe, stop at 66 Diner (66diner.com) for a burger or a classic milkshake.

BUILD YOUR TRIVIA KNOWLEDGE
WITH LOCAL TOURS

Albuquerque has two top tour companies whose outings are as informative and entertaining for visitors as they are for locals. It's hard to beat the enthusiasm and local knowledge of the purveyors of these companies, but it's always worth a try!

The multifaceted Albuquerque Tourism & Sightseeing Factory guides guests around town on a stucco-sided trolley, through downtown on ghost walks, and to the city's breweries on a party bike (to name a few). Its eighty-five-minute "Best of ABQ City Tours" by trolley has been called the best first thing to do in Albuquerque—an apt description since the tours are chock-full of local history and visit several neighborhoods, giving insider views of the city's personality.

You'll occasionally spot Duke City natives and Routes Bicycle Tours & Rentals owners Heather and Josh Arnold at the front of a pack of sunshine yellow and red cruiser bikes. Either they or members of their friendly team of guides lead cycling tours of the bosque daily. The company's themed outings include a Biking Bad tour and tours to local breweries, wineries, and chile-centric locales. The company also guides excursions to the Albuquerque International Balloon Fiesta, through Old Town's luminarias on Christmas Eve, and for Valentine's Day. Whichever tour you take, you're sure to return with new bits of local knowledge.

Neighborhood: Old Town
*Kid Friendly

**Albuquerque Tourism
& Sightseeing Factory**
800 Rio Grande Blvd. N.W.
(at Hotel Albuquerque)
(505) 200-2642
atsfworks.com

Routes Bicycle Tours & Rentals
2113 Charlevoix St. N.W.
(505) 933-5667
routesrentals.com

DANCE OVER
TO KESHET CENTER FOR THE ARTS

Shira Greenberg founded Keshet Dance as a professional repertory to bring contemporary dance to the Duke City. Since then, Keshet has grown into a multifaceted arts organization. It remains notable for its professional contemporary dance performances, as well as for its community-driven performances with dancers of many varieties, including those who use wheelchairs and other mobility devices. The Center for the Arts—and attached Ideas and Innovation Center—may be hidden in a warehouse district, but its studios, black-box spaces, and performance venues have become a draw thanks to visiting choreographers and dance groups from across the globe, resident theater troupes, and even adult and children's dance classes.

4121 Cutler Ave. N.E., (505) 224-9808, keshetarts.org

Neighborhood: Midtown
*Kid Friendly

TEST YOUR SHOPPING
CHOPS AT THE TURQUOISE MUSEUM

This small, privately owned museum explores all aspects of the color and stone that enraptures the Southwest. Members of the Lowry family, including the youngest, fifth generation, guide tours here. In August 2018, it's unveiling a new location in the Gertrude Zachary Castle, the former home of jewelry designer Gertrude Zachary and a notable landmark due to its unusual architecture. The museum entrance sets the stage with a stunning display: two hundred strings of turquoise hanging from the third story. The first room is also a showstopper with fifteen of the museum's world-class pieces, including the George Washington Stone, a chunk of turquoise cut into the shape of the founder's face on happy accident while preparing a piece for a hope chest. Subsequent rooms take you on a global tour, highlighting gems from around the world set in each country's distinctive art form. These pieces represent just a portion of J. C. Zachary Jr.'s (aka the King of Turquoise) collection. Don't miss the silversmithing and lapidary shop, where you can see cabochons being cut. Guides establish the gem's rarity and how frequently it is stabilized, synthetically recreated, and sometimes faked. Before you leave, you can browse the gift shop, which includes both natural (a key word!) and imitation turquoise, so you can practice your savvy shopping skills in a real-world environment.

400 Second St. S.W., turquoisemuseum.com

Neighborhood: Downtown
*Kid Friendly

RIDE
THE HIGH-WIRE BIKE AT ¡EXPLORA!

Riding the second-story, high-wire bike at this science center is the closest that many Albuquerqueans will ever get to being in a circus act. Riders pedal the bike along an easy, out-and-back route high above the other hands-on exhibits, including those devoted to gravity, water, air, and arts and crafts. By day, the science center may be aimed at kids, but once a month the center opens for an adults-only evening when the post-eighteen set can play in the bubbles without worrying about elbowing a toddler in an overly enthusiastic moment.

1701 Mountain Rd. N.W., (505) 224-8300, explora.us

Neighborhood: Old Town
*Kid Friendly

PERUSE
516 ARTS

This independent, nonprofit contemporary arts organization displays some of the most intriguing and thought-provoking visual art in the city. The gallery setting is perfect for the installations and multimedia creations frequently displayed here. In addition, 516 ARTS hosts a lively schedule of gallery talks, artist panels, workshops, and trunk shows. The organization has also made its mark on downtown's appearance with a series of murals on and near Central Avenue; duck inside the gallery to pick up a walking-tour map.

516 Central Ave. S.W., (505) 242-1445, 516arts.org

Neighborhood: Downtown

SWIM OVER TO THE
ABQ BIOPARK AQUARIUM

An aquarium in the desert? Yes, and a good one too. Exhibits cover habitats from the Rio Grande to the Gulf Coast. Visitors love the ray pool; however, the favorite is the 285,000-gallon shark tank. Aquarists (who care for the aquatic animals) scuba dive in the tank daily at 2 p.m. to hand-feed the manta rays with six-foot wingspans, the sharks, and Jimmy the sea turtle—a comical fellow who seems more golden retriever than turtle as he sidles up to the divers for a head scratch. A river otter exhibit recently opened, which stars two "nuisance" otters—they earned the title after stealing crustaceans from shrimp farmers in their native Louisiana—named Chaos and Mayhem. The Botanic Garden is on the same campus and is worth a visit for its elegant ceremonial gardens, Mediterranean conservatory, and Rio Grande farm exhibit. Don't miss the curandera garden, which pays homage to traditional healers with herbs and botanicals. The BUGarium is a hit with kids who don't mind the creepy crawlies, like leaf-cutter ants who traverse an overhead limb, giant peppered cockroaches, and desert centipedes.

2601 Central Ave. N.W., (505) 764-6200, cabq.gov

Neighborhood: Old Town
*Kid Friendly

BOTANIC GARDEN AGLOW

From approximately Thanksgiving through the New Year, the grounds of the gardens glitter at River of Lights, featuring all manner of animatronic and statuesque creatures (from stegosaurus to Pegasus) in lights. Check the schedule for the Victorian carolers who perform often during the popular event.

DRIVE
EL CAMINO REAL

Traveling the "royal road" is a trip through three hundred years of Southwestern heritage. El Camino Real de Tierra Adentro traveled a route nearly as long as its formal name, sixteen hundred miles from Mexico City, through what became the state of New Mexico. It was the earliest Euro-American trade route in the United States, and it brought as many Spanish colonists into today's New Mexico as it did goods. Today, you can drive sections of this historic route, including along NM 313 (aka Camino del Pueblo and El Camino Real) from the town of Bernalillo, which turns into Fourth Street in Albuquerque and extends to the south. Coronado Historic Site, described elsewhere in this book, is also along the route.

nps.gov/elca

Neighborhood: Bernalillo

LET WHIMSY TAKE OVER
AT TINKERTOWN MUSEUM

This is one of the most wonderfully wacky museums you'll ever encounter. Museum founder Ross Ward took more than forty years to carve and collect the mostly miniature wood-carved figures seen here—and to construct the unusual building made out of some fifty thousand glass bottles, as well as wagon wheels and horseshoes. Some fifteen hundred figurines are set in scenes including a mining town and a circus, and kids (or you) can press buttons to see the vignettes come to life.

121 Sandia Crest Rd., (505) 281-5233, tinkertown.com

Neighborhood: Sandia Park
*Kid Friendly

TIP
The museum is open April through October. Have quarters on hand—or get them when you buy your ticket—so you can play Otto, the one-man band, and learn your future from Esmerelda, the animatronic fortune-teller, á la Tom Hanks in *Big*.

MAKE YOUR WAY
TO MADRID

Driving the Turquoise Trail National Scenic Byway, on the east side of the Sandia Mountains, is the perfect day trip from the Duke City. The charming town of Madrid is a pleasant waypoint along the route. On Sundays, local motorcyclists flock in droves to the Mine Shaft Tavern for a burger and live music. The tavern is a throwback to the town's roots, but today there are more artists here than miners. You can spend an afternoon zigzagging across NM 14 to the galleries and eclectic shops that line the scenic route, including mainstays such as Johnsons of Madrid, Indigo Gallery, and Studio 14, the last of which represents more than twenty local artists. For a caffeinated pick-me-up—or a night's stay in the bed-and-breakfast—stop at Java Junction. Some of the best bites in town are the Southern-fried selections at the Hollar.

TIP
The Madrid Christmas Parade is one of the most eclectic small-town parades you'll ever see. Prepare yourself for vintage cars, bagpipes, and a Christmas yak.

MADRID HOT SPOTS

The Hollar
2849 NM 14, (505) 471-4821
thehollar.com

Java Junction
2855 NM 14, (505) 438-2772
java-junction.com

Johnsons of Madrid
2843 NM 14, (505) 471-1054

Indigo Gallery
2860 NM 14, Suite D, (505) 438-6202
indigoartgallery.com

Mine Shaft Tavern
2846 NM 14, (505) 473-0743
themineshafttavern.com

PICNIC
AT TASTY TUESDAY

Founded by a few food truck owners who wanted a weekly place to gather, this summertime event has become a popular family destination. Held at Hyder Park in the grassy knolls beneath a cottonwood canopy, the event is a picnic palooza. Attendees order from the revolving lineup of food trucks. (You'll often find the Supper Truck and Irrational Pie parked here.) Children gambol about in the grass as a live music performer plays, and in one corner of the park an alfresco yoga class salutes the sun.

Hyder Park, 700 Pershing Ave. S.E., facebook.com/TastyTuesdaysABQ

Neighborhood: Nob Hill
*Kid Friendly

TIP

The food trucks arrive at 4:30 p.m. Order your dinner early; the wait lengthens as the evening stretches on, and the trucks occasionally run out of menu items.

EXPLORE
ACOMA PUEBLO'S SKY CITY

Visiting the spectacular Sky City, an adobe Puebloan village perched on a sandstone bluff above the valley floor, makes for an extraordinary day trip. Inhabited since 1150 A.D., the pueblo is one of the longest continuously occupied communities in the United States. Visitors can't wander freely around Acoma Pueblo, so check out the Cultural Center and Haak'u Museum to purchase your tour ticket to Sky City. Although there are some five thousand members of Acoma Pueblo, about forty-five people reside year-round on the seventy-acre mesa top. A tour bus will transport you to the mesa's summit, and a guide will lead you among the traditional residences and past kivas (ceremonial chambers). A tour highlight is stepping inside San Esteban del Rey Mission, a National Historic Landmark. One of the largest churches of its kind, it still features the original altar and works of art that date to its 1629–1640 construction. Be sure to descend back to the cultural center via the stone staircase, which Puebloan ancestors once used as their sole access to and from their homes.

Fifty miles west of Albuquerque off I-40, (800) 747-0181, acomaskycity.org

*Kid Friendly

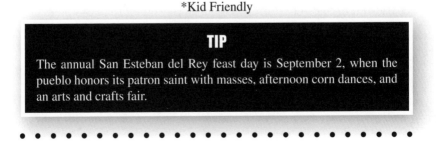

TIP
The annual San Esteban del Rey feast day is September 2, when the pueblo honors its patron saint with masses, afternoon corn dances, and an arts and crafts fair.

TOUR
THE TAMARIND INSTITUTE

Although it may be below the radar of many Albuquerqueans, the Tamarind Institute has a world-class reputation in the art of lithography. A division of the College of Fine Arts at the University of New Mexico, the institute runs a second-story gallery space that mounts a handful of shows each year. But this is primarily a working print shop that runs a professional program, sponsoring eight students and two apprentices a year who earn their master printer certificates. The program also facilitates the work of invited artists who, though celebrated in their respective media, may be creating a lithograph for the first time. Artists who have worked at the institute during its more than fifty-year history (it was founded in 1960 in Los Angeles and moved to Albuquerque in 1970) include former associate director Clinton Adams and former technical director Garo Antreasian, Hung Liu, and Jim Dine. The institute offers ninety-minute tours on the first Friday of most months that guide you through the professional and student sides of the print shop and demonstrate the lithography process, in which an artist creates an image—in this case, on a stone—then inks the plate and pulls an impression.

2500 Central Ave. S.E., (505) 277-3901, tamarind.unm.edu

Neighborhood: University

• •

TIP

If you want to explore the institute's full archives, the University of New Mexico Art Museum, described elsewhere in this book, keeps an archive of every print created since the institute's founding. The archives can be viewed by appointment.

PLUG INTO THE
OLD TOWN TREE LIGHTING

Albuquerque's Plaza Don Luis may not be Rockefeller Center, but it comes pretty close when the fifty-five-foot tree is alight there each December. The tree is actually made up of 155 smaller trees assembled to look like a towering pine. It's then hung with twenty thousand sparkling lights, bows, and snowflake ornaments. Henry Aceves, past president of the Old Town Merchants Association and longtime Old Town business owner, along with his wife, Karen, established the tree lighting as a community tradition. Plaza Don Luis, where the tree is assembled, was named after Henry's father. Although Aceves passed away, the tree lighting continues as a favorite community tradition. It coincides with the Old Town Shop and Stroll, when neighborhood stores stay open late for holiday shopping.

Plaza Don Luis, cabq.gov, albuquerqueoldtown.com

Neighborhood: Old Town
*Kid Friendly

WATCH THE CORRALES
FOURTH OF JULY PARADE

This pastoral village, just north of Albuquerque, presents a charming Independence Day parade. Anyone is welcome to join, whether two or four legged. Town residents promenade with their dogs, alpacas, donkeys, rabbits, and even chickens—all decked out in red, white, and blue for the occasion, of course. You'll also see vintage trucks and bagpipe bands—and the slightly less baritone kazoo bands. Bring your own chair and pick a spot along Corrales Road, the main thoroughfare; after the parade, join the festivities at La Entrada Park.

corralesjuly4.com

Neighborhood: Corrales
*Kid Friendly

TIP

Check Corrales's community calendar for other events throughout the year. The October Harvest Festival and May studio tour are also prime times to explore this charming community.

CHECK OUT
THE ERNIE PYLE LIBRARY

Pulitzer Prize–winning journalist Ernie Pyle became a household name during World War II thanks to his accounts of ordinary people in rural America and soldiers on the frontlines. In 1940, he adopted Albuquerque as his home when he and his wife constructed their 1,145-square-foot house in Nob Hill. An early embedded journalist, Pyle was killed in 1945 by a sniper's bullet on the island of Iwo Jima, but his writings inspired the story of G.I. Joe, which has grown to encompass movies, comic books, and action figures. His quaint five-room home has a second life too—as a branch of the Albuquerque/Bernalillo County Library system. With books lining every wall, Pyle would likely be proud of his home's transformation. The library memorializes Pyle in historic photographs and a few artifacts, like monogrammed ashtrays, goggles he used through his reporting in the World War II Africa campaign, and a replica of a two-headed lion ring he wore daily on the battlefield.

900 Girard Blvd. S.E., (505) 265-2065; abqlibrary.org/erniepyle

Neighborhood: Nob Hill
*Kid Friendly

TAKE A GHOST TOUR
OF OLD TOWN

Whether you're ready to see a specter or just skeptical, this tour is an enjoyable way to learn about the city's past. Guided by Tours of Old Town, this walk through Albuquerque's founding neighborhood will take you past the ill-chosen former location of the town graveyard, the previous home of the undertaker, High Noon Restaurant and Saloon, and down "Scarlett's Alley" to hear chill-inducing ghost stories. The tales, which include mention of trappers, Confederate soldiers, prostitutes, and blue-collar workers, reflect the many phases of the neighborhood's past—beginning when Albuquerque was just four blocks across.

Plaza Don Luis, 303 Romero St. N.W., Suite N120
(505) 246-8687, toursofoldtown.com

Neighborhood: Old Town

TIP
Reservations for the nightly tours are required. Tours of Old Town also offers once-a-month moonlight tours at a later time. Spook Troop tours for junior ghost hunters aged six to twelve offer softer versions of the ghost stories.

SHOPPING AND FASHION

BROWSE
OLD TOWN

A trip to this tree-lined plaza is first on many visitors' lists—particularly because it's the city's founding neighborhood—and there are plenty of tourist-focused trinket shops to prove it. But among the 150 shops there are plenty of galleries and boutiques too. You may also shop from the Native American craftspeople who lay out blankets with their wares on the plaza. You'll easily spend a few hours wandering down cobblestone pathways and through small courtyards off the plaza, such as the one at Poco a Poco Patio.

albuquerqueoldtown.com

Neighborhood: Old Town
*Kid Friendly

OLD TOWN SHOPPING LIST

Albuquerque Photographers' Gallery: This artist co-op includes some of the city's best artists—and you'll find stunning pictures of the state's landscapes and people here.

Plaza Don Luis, 303 Romero St. N.W., Suite 208
(505) 244-9195, abqphotographersgallery.com

Church Street Cafe: This restaurant in a historic adobe serves authentic—and delicious—New Mexican fare.

2111 Church St. N.W., (505) 247-8522, churchstreetcafe.com

Matí: For contemporary jewelry, the sparkling opals and diamonds at Matí by international design house Kabana may catch your eye.

201 Romero St. N.W., (505) 244-1595, matijewelers.com

Tanner Chaney Galleries: In business since 1875, this gallery has fine Native American jewelry, pottery, and rugs. It also offers a healthy collection of estate and pawn jewelry, which provides fine opportunities for bargains.

323 Romero St. N.W., (505) 247-2242, tannerchaney.com

GET HEARTY AND HALE
AT LOCAL GROWERS MARKETS

The Downtown Growers' Market and the Rail Yards Market are the city's top stops for fresh-from-the-field produce. The downtown market, held on Saturdays, has a larger number of participating farmers, with regulars such as Skarsgard Farms (operators of the state's largest community-supported agriculture share) and Wagner Farms. At the Rail Yards Market, held on Sundays in the revitalized blacksmith shop of the once-derelict Rail Yards, producers such as Vecinos del Bosque keep Albuquerqueans stocked up on arugula, carrots, and tomatoes, to name a few. The markets also sell prepared foods. Craftspeople set up shop here too, selling homemade soaps and lotions, jewelry, and pottery. The markets aren't just places to shop; they're also community gathering spots for neighbors and friends. At the downtown market, families sprawl on blankets in the grass of Robinson Park and kids kick up their heels to live bluegrass music. At the Rail Yards Market, bystanders can watch—or join in with—belly dancers or folklorico dancers at the community stage and watch a children's play or listen to poetry on the main stage.

Downtown Growers' Market
Eighth St. and Central Ave., (505) 252-2959, downtowngrowers.com

Rail Yards Market
777 First St. S.W., (505) 600-1109, railyardsmarket.org

Neighborhoods: Downtown and Barelas
*Kid Friendly

PICK UP A BAUBLE
AT GERTRUDE ZACHARY JEWELRY

Although groundbreaking businesswoman Gertrude Zachary (1937–2013) passed away, she left a brightly colored stamp on Southwestern jewelry. She and her daughter, Erica Hatchell, who has also taken up the design mantle, are known for contemporary Southwestern creations in a field that men long dominated. Zachary particularly enjoyed bold statement pieces—from chunky turquoise necklaces to eye-catching coral cuffs. Her stores (one in Nob Hill, one in Old Town) offer so many glittering choices, it may be difficult to pick just one.

Old Town: 1501 Lomas Blvd. N.W., (505) 247-4442
Nob Hill: 3300 Central Ave. S.E., (505) 766-4700
gertrudezachary.com

Neighborhoods: Old Town and Nob Hill

HOBNOB
IN NOB HILL

Planned by Colonel D. K. B. Sellers, Nob Hill was platted in 1916—just four years after New Mexico became a state. The real-estate developer encouraged residents to move beyond the city's core, in his words "out of the low zone into the ozone," since the neighborhood was then on the city's outskirts. At Carlisle Boulevard, Sellers spied a steep slope that struck him as similar to that of San Francisco's Nob Hill and decided to adopt that more famous district's name. A hundred years on, the neighborhood still feels young, with more than 250 independent shops, restaurants, galleries, and bars unfolding from Central Avenue. The best part: everything's within walking distance. So park the car and enjoy.

route66central.com

Neighborhood: Nob Hill

NOB HILL SHOPPING LIST

IMEC
Jewelry is wearable art, particularly here at the International Metalsmithing Exhibition Center.

101 Amherst Dr. S.E., (505) 265-8352
shopimec.com

Izzy Martin Menswear
This hip men's clothing boutique outfits some of the best-dressed gents in town.

103 Amherst Dr. S.E., (505) 232-9223
izzymartin.com

Mariposa Gallery

This contemporary crafts gallery curates a collection that lives up to its tag line: curiouser and curiouser. Pulling from its stable of represented artists and guests, the gallery also presents monthly exhibits.

3500 Central Ave. S.E.
(505) 268-6828, mariposa-gallery.com

Retail Therapy ABQ

Shop brands that give back and local-pride clothing and accessories at this mom-and-daughter shop.

107 Amherst Dr. S.E., (505) 219-3761
retailtherapyabq.com

Toad Road

A men's and women's clothing boutique, Toad Road offers brand names and items from local designers with a dash of vintage finds for good measure.

3503 Central Ave. N.E., (505) 255-4212

HISTORICAL HIGHLIGHTS

Check out these buildings while browsing.

Nob Hill Shopping Center

Designed by noted architect Louis Hesselden, this shopping center boasts the iconic "Nob Hill" sign, and it was designed with a mixture of Territorial Revival and Moderne elements. Today, it's home to La Montañita Co-Op and Scalo, a northern Italian grill, among others.

3500 Central Ave. S.E.

Monte Vista Fire Station Restaurant

There's truth in advertising in this restaurant's name: the building was formerly a fire station. Architect Ernst Blumenthal incorporated Spanish-Pueblo Revival elements in this structure's design. It was built in 1936 under the WPA.

3201 Central Ave. N.E., (505) 255-2424

Immanuel Presbyterian Church

Renowned architect John Gaw Meem designed this working church in 1949. It exudes what came to be known as the Territorial Revival style.

114 Carlisle Blvd. S.E., (505) 265-7628
rt66church.com

Kellys Brew Pub

On summer evenings, Kellys patio is packed with revelers sipping craft beer and noshing on nachos. At one time, however, there were more Fords than frolickers on this patio. In 1939, Ralph Jones commissioned a Ford dealership and service station to be the home of the Jones Motor Company. The building, a fine example of the Streamline Moderne architectural style, is now listed on the National Register of Historic Places.

3222 Central Ave. S.E., (505) 262-2739
kellysbrewpub.com

FLIP OPEN
RED PLANET BOOKS & COMICS

This is one of only a handful of bookstores in North America devoted to titles by Native American authors. It becomes one of a kind with its focus on comics, games, and action figures by indigenous artists. In the store, you'll find children's books from authors like Sherman Alexie and Native American comic books like the well-known *Tribal Force* and *Super Indian*. It's the creation of Native Realities, a media company founded in Albuquerque that publishes and distributes Native American comic books. You'll find the company's own publications too, like a comic book anthology and a collection celebrating World War II code talkers. (Code talkers, primarily Navajo tribal members from Arizona and New Mexico, created an unbreakable code in their language that helped the United States gain the upper hand in the war.) The store highlights the amazing work of Native and indigenous artists in pop culture.

1002 Park Ave. S.W., (505) 361-1182, redplanetbooksabq.com

Neighborhood: Downtown
*Kid Friendly

TIP

The store doubles as the
headquarters for Indigenous
Comic Con. Founded in 2016,
the convention celebrates Native
Americans' contributions to comic
books, superhero movies, and science
fiction with panels, signings,
and costume contests.

indigenouscomiccon.com

ATTEND A LITERARY
EVENT AT BOOKWORKS

This locally owned indie bookstore has a calendar socialites would envy: it hosts four to five hundred events annually. In 1984, founder Nancy Rutland opened the bookstore with the aim of creating a literary meeting place. New owners Danielle Foster and Wyatt Wegrzyn, both longtime employees, took over the business in 2011. Since then, they've expanded the store's presence as a "third place"—a locale between work and home for like-minded people to meet and discuss not only literature but also current events and social issues. Its monthly lineup includes author readings and talks, especially with writers of color or those who have traditionally been at the margins, as well as book club meetings and writing workshops. Children aren't left out; its Thursday morning story time has been a store tradition since Bookworks opened. In addition to stocking new and used books by national authors, it keeps a hearty helping of titles by New Mexico and Southwest writers of every genre.

4022 Rio Grande Blvd. N.W., (505) 344-8139, bkwrks.com

Neighborhood: North Valley
*Kid Friendly (depending on the author)

Another Indie Bookstore Favorite: Page One Books
5850 Eubank Blvd. N.E., Suite B41, (505) 294-2026, page1book.com

Neighborhood: Northeast Heights

TIP

Check the schedule for A Word with Writers, a biannual event featuring authors in conversation with each other that doubles as a fundraiser for the Albuquerque Library Foundation.

MAKE A PILGRIMAGE
TO SKIP MAISEL'S INDIAN JEWELRY

This go-to spot for Native American jewelry and pottery has reached landmark status in the city. Maurice Maisel started the store in 1923 and moved it to its current location in 1939, in a building designed by noted architect John Gaw Meem. You may be here to shop, but before you get to the bargains inside, linger in the T-shaped entrance. Here, contractor John McDowell set a thunderbird of crushed turquoise and coral in the terrazzo floor. Above the window displays, murals created by students of Dorothy Dunn, of the Santa Fe Indian School, depict Navajo, deer, butterfly, and corn dancers; an antelope hunt; and other cultural vignettes. Inside, most of this wholesaler's prices are half off retail, so you'll find great deals on Navajo, Jemez, and Acoma pottery, as well as traditional Southwestern jewelry in every hue, from multistrand turquoise heishis to coral squash blossom necklaces.

510 Central Ave. S.W., (505) 242-6526, skipmaisels.com

Neighborhood: Downtown

Albuquerque public art

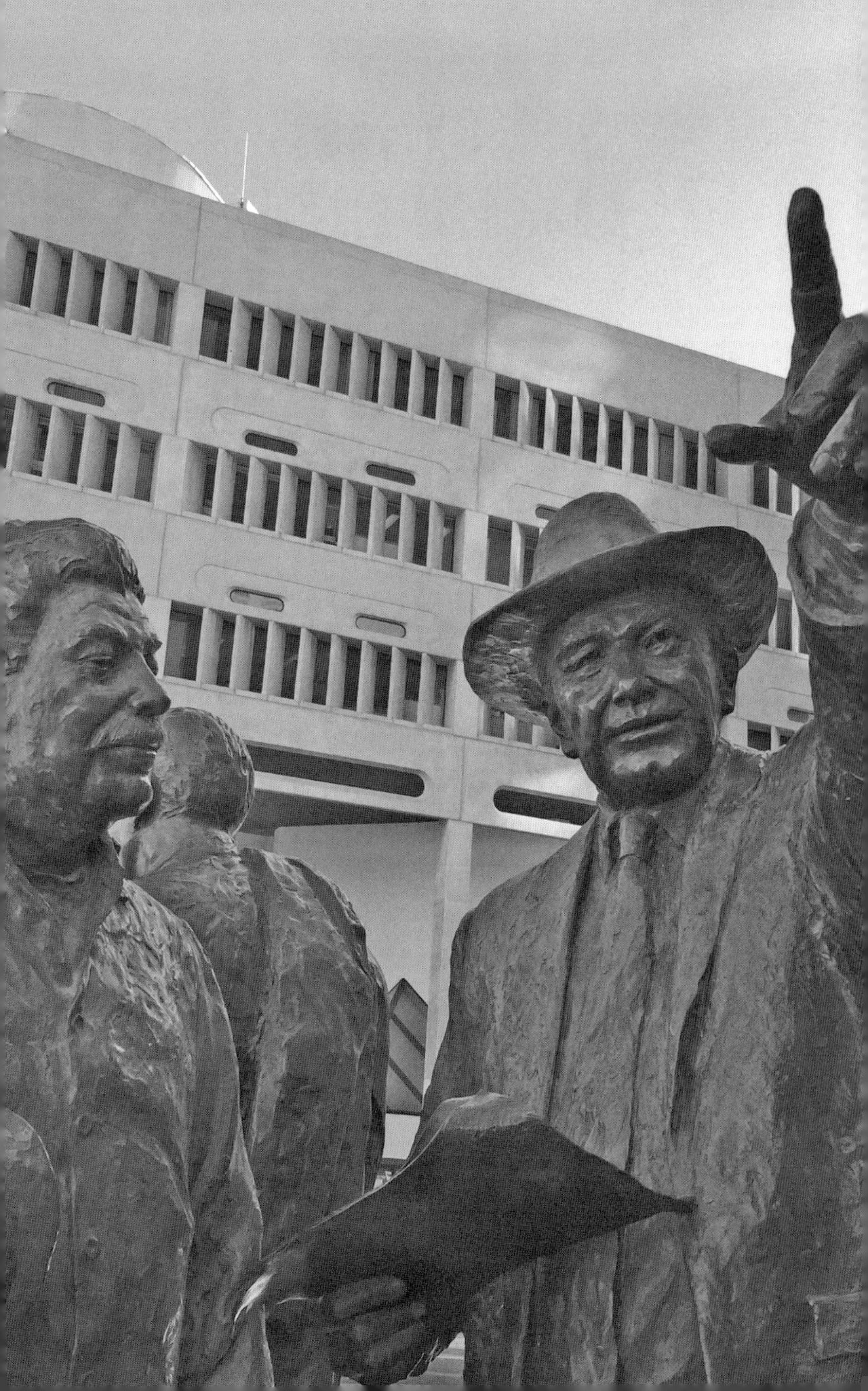

SUGGESTED ITINERARIES

BOTTOMS UP

ART, MUSIC, AND THEATER LOVERS

LOCAL CULTURE SEEKERS

DATE NIGHT

FAMILIES

GIRLS' DAY OR NIGHT OUT

GREAT OUTDOORS

HISTORY BUFFS

LOCAVORES

ACTIVITIES BY SEASON

FALL

SPRING

SUMMER

WINTER

Mister Car Wash
(a filming location for *Breaking Bad*)

INDEX

• •

Kasha-Katuwe Tent Rocks
National Monument